THE
MASTER KEY

Unlock Your Influence
& Succeed in Negotiation

LUDOVIC TENDRON

Copyright © 2020 by Ludovic Tendron

All rights reserved. No part of this publication may be reproduced, distributed, or transmitted in any form or by any means, including photocopying, recording, or other electronic or mechanical methods, without the prior written permission of the publisher, except in the case of brief quotations embodied in critical reviews and certain other noncommercial uses permitted by copyright law. For permission requests, write to the publisher, addressed "Attention: Permissions Coordinator," at the address below.

www.ludovic.online

Ordering Information:
Quantity sales. Special discounts are available on quantity purchases by corporations, associations, and others.
Please contact info@ludovic.asia | +65 9786 6484

Printed by KDP Print in the United States of America

Ludovic Tendron

The Master Key, Unlock Your Influence & Success in Negotiations

ISBN 978-0-578-61111-2

1. Negotiation. 2. Negotiating skills. 3. Influencing skills. 4. Conflict resolution. 5. Influencer. 6. Psychology of negotiation. 7. Personal Power. 8. Persuasion.

First Edition

14 13 12 11 10 / 10 9 8 7 6 5 4 3 2 1

*To the great women of my life
(Grace, Charlie, my mother, my grandmother and my sisters),
and to those who strive to become better negotiators ...*

⌈CONTENTS⌋

INTRODUCTION 1
  We Always Negotiate 1
  The Need to Be a Good Negotiator 4
  The Cost of Bad Negotiation 6
  The Neglected Factors 8
  Take the High Road 9

CHAPTER ONE: The Essence of Negotiation 13
  1 Cutting the Cake 14
  2 The Choice to Trust 16
  3 Gaining Leverage 18
  4 The Search for a Fair Deal 20
  5 The Best Negotiators 24

CHAPTER TWO: The Art of Preparation 29
  6 Gather Useful Data 30
  7 Your Attitude Makes a Big Difference 33
  8 Be Focused 37
  9 Learn to Discipline Your Mind 42
  10 Self-Awareness: A Vital Attribute 46
  11 First Impressions 49

CHAPTER THREE: Evolving in the Modern World 53
  12 The Evil of Our Time 54
  13 Technology Changes Us 57

14 The World Is a Global Village 62
15 Global Mindset Required 66

CHAPTER FOUR: About Human Nature 75

16 Mind Body Language 76
17 Develop Emotional Intelligence 80
18 These Shortcuts We Take 87
19 The Gender Impact 94
20 The Group Effect 100
21 The Status Motivator 104
22 Why Integrity Pays Better 106
23 The Risk Factor 111

CHAPTER FIVE: Influencing Others 115

24 Build Rapport 116
25 The Road to Persuasion 123

CHAPTER SIX: Reach Your Peak 135

26 Develop a Personal Brand 136
27 Set the Bar 143
28 Those Personal Traits 148

CHAPTER SEVEN: Timeless Principles 163

29 The Power of Silence 165
30 Practice Food Sharing 168
31 Be Connected 176
32 Be a Giver, Not a Taker 178
33 Keep Your Promises 179

INTRODUCTION

⌈We Always Negotiate⌋

In the heyday of his activity, John D. Rockefeller said, 'the ability to deal with people is as purchasable a commodity as sugar or coffee. And I will pay more for that ability than for any other under the sun.' Wouldn't you suppose that every college in the land would conduct courses to develop the highest-priced ability under the sun? But if there is just one practical, common sense course of that kind given for adults in even one college in the land, it has escaped my attention up to the present writing.

—Dale Carnegie[1]

Like it or not, human relationships require negotiation. When we talk about the way we live with others, we're talking about negotiation. Any society, from tribal communities in the Amazon rain forest to social club members in a bustling metropolis, results from negotiations. Individuals have banded together and agreed, whether explicitly or implicitly, to act by a prescribed set of rules and to exchange goods and services on the basis of agreed-upon values.

Negotiation is often considered a formal activity, taking place in a meeting room, at a diplomatic summit, etc. However, we negotiate every time we shop, socialize, and, unless we live alone, every day at home with our loved

---

[1] Dale Carnegie, *How to Win Friends and Influence People* (New York: Simon & Schuster, 1981), XVI.

ones. We can negotiate for our own interests, those of others, or act as an intermediary between two parties.

Humans are born negotiators. The second an infant learns that they can cry to get fed, they learn the power of bargaining. Even though we are born to be negotiators, many of us aren't very good at it. Negotiation is often learned on the job, and we frequently let our emotions control our decisions or actions.

The world is one big chess board, and everyone's playing. Unfortunately, not all of us know all the rules or how best to apply them. Because most of us don't realize the ubiquity of negotiation and don't possess a reliable key to discern its sometimes-puzzling rules, we are at a disadvantage when dealing with master players. What we don't know could mean the difference between success and failure.

Negotiation skills are a valuable tool to influence others as well as to resolve conflicts. We humans create a lot of conflicts. Such conflicts range in scale from international clashes to interpersonal tension. Yet, conflict is not universally bad. From social conflict progress can emerge.

Laws, cultures, and organized societies have mandated solutions to a great many conflicts, but we know that these rules can maintain the status quo or keep peace insofar as people agree to follow them. The more powerful people are, the less inclined they are to follow the same rules as the rest of us.[2]

Conflict of interest is as inevitable and as ubiquitous as negotiation. Two parties in a room often hold differing views and have different goals and aims. Scarce supply, growing demand, and unequal allocation of resources draw parties to compete and protect their own personal interests.

If you work in corporate management, you live the truth of negotiation and conflict in daily life. During many years serving corporations, I consider that top managers spend at least three-fourths of their time negotiating. This is every day, at all levels.

---

[2] Gerben A. Van Kleef, Astrid C. Homan, Catrin Finkenauer, Seval Gündemir, and Eftychia Stamkou. "Breaking the Rules to Rise to Power: How Norm Violators Gain Power in the Eyes of Others." *Social Psychological and Personality Science* 2, 2011 2(5): 500–507.

The human race has experienced ages and cultures where compromise with others could be seen as a sign of weakness. For a long time, domination and physical strength were necessary for survival. Now, however, we live in a world where negotiation and compromise are indispensable skills, even an art. Donald Trump's *The Art of the Deal* takes such a perspective in its title, and *Shark Tank* has turned the art of negotiation into an iconic television show.

Negotiation, far from being a sign of weakness in the modern landscape, is essential for success. Remember Trump telling everyone that he was the world's best dealmaker? Enough Americans believed it to vote him into office. They saw his ability to make deals as an essential asset for a world leader. Whether he managed to keep these promises is another story, but his success in winning an election demonstrates the value people place in the power of negotiation.

There aren't many worthwhile memorable books on the subject although many have been written on it. Negotiation is not something you easily find in a list of required college courses. Even though I studied law, I didn't start off any more informed about negotiation skills. In law school, I learned everything you'd want to know, and plenty you wouldn't, about how to draft a contract, but I learned nothing about how to influence people or become emotionally intelligent. These are subjects that law books don't tackle. Many of us rely on our technical expertise to negotiate, forgetting that negotiation is primarily a question of psychology and understanding of human nature.

If you want to master negotiations, gain influence, and build valuable relationships, this book is for you. It will show you negotiation in a much broader sense. The real truth about negotiation is far from the bag of tricks some "experts" try to sell you, and that you promptly forget as soon you are caught in the vortex of emotional transactions. In these pages, we will take the higher road for practical and valuable reasons. I offer you a master key to open doors of opportunity.

⌈The Need to Be a Good Negotiator⌋

> I may hazard a guess that there is perhaps no employment in all Majesty's service more difficult to discharge than that of negotiation. It demands all penetration, all the dexterity, all the suppleness a man can possess. It requires a widespread understanding and knowledge, and above.
>
> —François de Callières[3]

Despite conflicts, humans remain social animals. Survival and reproduction have long demanded negotiation in one form or another. Acceptance into a group requires an ability to navigate relationships.

Some animals live the majority of their lives alone. They have company only when competing for a mate or raising their young. Humans are not solitary creatures. We need one another, and we require the cooperation of others to achieve our objectives. Civilization emerges from and thrives through negotiation.

Over the last few centuries, industrialization has led mass migration from rural to urban living. More and more people live closely to one another. Globalization and new technologies have increased the phenomena. By 2050, the United Nations expects that 68 percent of the world's population will be living in urban areas. Cities of more than ten million people will increase in number.[4] They shelter complex and competitive social environments. They're centers of society, culture, and commerce, currently generating 80 percent of the world's GDP.

This denser concentration of people has naturally led to big changes in the way we behave. High population concentration leads to a greater number

---

[3] François de Callières, *On the Manner of Negotiating with Princes* (Paris: Mercure Galant, Paris, 1716), 9.

[4] The United Nations News, "68% of the world population projected to live in urban areas by 2050, says UN," May 16, 2018.

of interactions but also to more tensions, stress, and frustration. These unfortunate by-products of the modern world put a strain on social relations, and lead to greater dissension and governments responding by exerting a more extensive control. In densely populated areas, people are forced to cooperate, but many feel a more pronounced need to protect their personal interests.

Skills in negotiating, especially the skill for emotional intelligence, are indispensable tools if one hopes to thrive in this rapidly evolving environment. It has always been useful to be knowledgeable, listen well, and speak well, but this is not sufficient to establish a real and lasting influence.

You can be a brilliant financier, engineer, or doctor. However, your expertise in a particular field doesn't necessarily make you a brilliant negotiator. You've probably noticed that the experts are often not the ones enjoying the highest positions in the business world. Such positions go to the great negotiators – those who know how to influence, lead, and manage others, and who have used their negotiation abilities to climb higher. The best leaders surround themselves with experts, and they know how to pull the right strings. According to Dale Carnegie, *"15% of one's financial success is due to one's technical knowledge and about 85% is due to skills in human engineering – to personality and the ability to lead people."*[5] I can't agree with him more.

Maybe you have an idea that will change the world, or you've developed a truly essential product. Yet, without negotiation your work will only get you so far. In the end, you'll have to convince someone to buy what you're selling. To do that well, you need to master negotiation.

---

[5] Dale Carnegie, *How to Win Friends and Influence People* (New York: Simon & Schuster, 1981), XVI.

The Cost of Bad Negotiation

Oftentimes to win us to our harm, the instruments of darkness tell us truths; win us with honest trifles, to betray's in deepest consequence.

—William Shakespeare[6]

Nikola Tesla (1856-1943) had an idea that did change the world. He invented a truly essential technology, one we use every day. He could have become the richest man on earth, the world's first billionaire, had he been a better negotiator.

Before Tesla developed alternating current (AC), power could only travel a maximum of one mile from the plant. In those days, Thomas Edison's direct current (DC) technology was the standard, and it lit up cities throughout the United States. Yet, DC was cumbersome and expensive. Thanks to Tesla's invention, power could travel over much longer distances, and more sparsely populated areas could receive the benefits of electricity.

Tesla, perhaps more than any other figure, ushered in the worldwide revolution of easily accessible power. It ought to have made him a fortune, but he sold his patents to George Westinghouse, an American businessman, for a mere 60,000 dollars in cash and royalties. Westinghouse, while under financial pressure and bad press from Edison, even convinced Tesla to give up his royalties.

Tesla was sure that his brilliance would lead him to even greater success, but he was wrong. Though his ideas won him famous investors like J. P. Morgan, most of his successive schemes never materialized in his lifetime, and none had the world-changing impact of his AC motor. He died a poor man, alone in a hotel in New York. In the meantime, George Westinghouse's business flourished.

---

[6] William Shakespeare, *Macbeth* (Cambridge University Press, 1997), Act I, Scene III, 116.

Had Tesla been wiser, he could have requested to delay his royalty payments, until the company could afford to have it lifted, make their waiver conditional, or just decrease them. Tesla didn't pursue any of these options and his business went downhill.

A single bad negotiation can have a ripple effect. Your peers can lose confidence in you, and it can undermine a reputation you've spent years building. In some cultures, like those of Korea and Japan, errors in negotiation can result in a substantial loss of face. Working in hospitality, I saw people sidelined and even sacked for negotiating bad hotel deals. A bad deal leaves a stain on others' impression of you – one that isn't easily washed off.

Bad negotiations can affect far more than yourself. Entire nations, even the whole world, can suffer as the result of a poorly constructed agreement. The Second World War was the consequence, in part, of bad negotiations. At the end of World War I, Germany was severely punished for its role in the conflict. In addition to taking full responsibility for the war, having its army hobbled and part of its territory given to neighboring states, Germany was required to shoulder most of the cost of reconstruction, which sent its economy into a tailspin and made its culture a breeding ground for extremism. The promise of reparations was a short-term win for the winners of WWI, but the effects of the extreme punitive actions destabilized the geopolitical climate in the long term and set the stage for a sequel.

In the business world, we find many examples of disastrous deals with far-reaching and expensive consequences. In the case of Apple and Samsung, both parties lost because of their stubborn unwillingness to sit down together, negotiate, and settle. Apple first sued Samsung in 2011 for copying the patented designs of several of its mobile devices. By the next year, the two tech giants were tangled together in over 50 lawsuits across the globe. Billions of dollars were at stake, but by the time the two parties finally reached an agreement in June of 2018, after sinking so much time and money battling in the courtroom, Apple as the victor was left with negligible financial gain. The real winners were probably the lawyers.

⌈The Neglected Factors⌋

> We labor unceasingly to adorn and preserve this imaginary existence, and neglect the real.
>
> —Blaise Pascal[7]

We often think we are better negotiators than we are and that we know how to best defend our own interests. We tend to value our own opinions more highly than those of others and judge ourselves more favorably than we should. This is what psychologists call the "self-service bias."

Negotiation requires emotional intelligence and a working knowledge of human psychology. It calls for an understanding of the brain's mechanics and how we make decisions, taking into consideration cultural diversity, context, gender, etc. Unlike a skilled negotiator, most of us are unaware of the cognitive biases that affect our worldviews. Such biases are difficult to spot, but an awareness of both your own and your counterpart's biases may mean the difference between successful and poor outcomes.

Many of us still see negotiation as a verbal game. However, negotiation is so much more than words. It is a full-body activity where physiology, body language, energy, and attitude (to name a few) play an important role. Good negotiators need a firm grasp of all these elements to be effective.

If you want to be a master negotiator, you must approach the craft with the mentality of an athlete: negotiation is an art, but it is also a discipline. You need control of your mind and your body. You need a capacity to enter the flow and easily adapt when the unforeseen arises. Just like athletes, we are in constant competition, but for promotions, markets, clients, bonuses, resources, recognition, and more. To come out on top, you must perform at your peak.

---

[7] Blaise Pascal, *Pensées* (Woodstock, Ontario, Canada: Devoted Publishing, 2018), 31.

Many negotiators neglect to prepare well. To run a marathon or climb Mount Everest, there are necessary concrete steps to take. The same truth applies to negotiation. Negotiation should, whenever possible, subtly begin before you ever start pitching a sale. You should foster a state of mind in the other party that will allow them to be receptive to your ideas and proposals. Something as seemingly inconsequential as sharing a meal can make a foundational difference, for instance.

⌈Take the High Road⌋

> However tight things are, you still need to have the big picture at the forefront of your mind.
>
> —Richard Branson[8]

Many books have been written on negotiation. They take a variety of perspectives, but many either fail to be practical in the long term, don't address the issue in adequate depth or breadth, or neglect to discuss the most basic principles of psychology.

Knowing oneself is as important as knowing others. Yet, some authors prefer to focus outward on how to modify certain behavior patterns in others. It is certainly important to put ourselves in another's shoes, but, if we're courageous enough to look inward, we often discover that we're the problem or part of it.

Teaching negotiation is not like teaching a boxing protégé jabbing techniques and strikes. This would be underestimating important factors that affect negotiation. We should broaden our mindset and look at the bigger picture. Some authors might tell you that it's never a good idea to accept a first offer. Others might provide a detailed blueprint for how to deal with angry negotiators. However, so many different factors come into play during

---

[8] Richard Branson, *Losing My Virginity* (United Kingdom: Virgin Books, 2009), 400.

a negotiation. It is risky to set strict rules and lose agility to respond to reality. The higher the number of set rules, the lower the likelihood that these rules can be remembered. The solution is to elevate your thinking to be able to perform efficiently in all circumstances.

The Master Key contains general principles – laws that are reliable and broadly applicable – that improve your chances of success in a variety of negotiations. It is designed to offer advice that stays with the reader, advice that's applicable regardless of age, gender, or culture.

Our world is rapidly evolving, but negotiation is as old as time. Contracts have been negotiated since the dawn of recorded history. In fact, the need to keep a record of such negotiations and transactions was one of the reasons ancient peoples began writing in the first place. Now, new modes of communication are emerging, and understanding how to negotiate using new technologies has become critical to perform.

When tackling negotiation, it is important to explore recent scientific work to understand human interactions in a more concrete, objective light. The business world, perhaps blinded by the desire for profit, sometimes ignores these findings. It fails to implement principles that have proven to be effective. I have decades of experience, and a wealth of personal stories that I'll share, to support the claims made in this book. However, the information in *The Master Key* isn't merely based on my opinion, it draws from studies in a variety of fields to demonstrate that the laws of negotiation are grounded in science and fact.

More than a century ago, people began to employ the scientific method to understand their behavior. Progress on this front has revealed many of the secrets of human nature. I've spent years researching how and why people behave the way they do in the context of negotiation. In this book I distill what I've learned into a readable and concise message that you can use to develop powerful negotiating skills and mindset.

The Master Key will teach you how to develop a global mindset to negotiate anywhere. In an interconnected world with open borders, the ability to build bridges between your culture and that of others is a pivotal asset.

Developing an open mindset can help to compensate for any lack of past cultural experiences.

The Master Key will equip you with the tools to establish rapport with others and to trigger a positive reaction by employing subtle, simple cues. You'll learn to train your mind to be organized and agile and to exude confidence in your language, tone, and demeanor. You'll learn the values of nonverbal communication, positive energy, self-awareness, and many others to achieve the best possible outcome.

In closing, I'd like to address my purpose for writing this book. Negotiation is definitely key to climbing the social ladder. While successful negotiation leads to gains, it also leads to a more meaningful life. If we could all negotiate better, we would be cooperating toward a brighter and more harmonious future in this world. When you operate with this mindset, you appear more authentic, more open minded, more creative, and more likable. History produced many great negotiators, all with their own style, and these attributes are often a common denominator among them. Simon Sinek, in his famous Ted Talk[9] concurs with this vision when he says:

> *Great, inspiring leaders in the world think, act, and communicate the exact same way… Very few people know why they do what they do. And by "why" I don't mean "to make a profit." That's the result. By "why," I mean, "What's your purpose? What's your cause? What's your belief? Why does your organization exist? Why do you get out of bed in the morning? And why should anyone care?" Inspired leaders think, act, and communicate from the inside out.*

My hope is that *The Master Key* will help readers on the path to self-improvement and greater personal success, but also shift the emphasis from personal gain to interpersonal elevation.

---

[9] Simon Sinek, "How Great Leaders Inspire Action," TEDx Puget Sound, September 2009, 17:50, www.ted.com/talks/simon_sinek_how_great_leaders_inspire_action/.

CHAPTER ONE:
The Essence of Negotiation

How many of us know what the word truly means and where it comes from? This may seem like a pedantic exercise to some, but to grasp this concept in its essence, starting from the beginning is important.

The word "negotiation" comes from the Old French *"negociacion,"* drawn from the Latin words *"negotiari"* ("the act of doing business") and *"negotium"* ("occupation"). In Latin, *"otium"* means "leisure." *"Negotium,"* then, would indicate a lack of leisure.

In ancient Rome, citizens were divided into a number of classes: (1) patricians, the ruling class, didn't engage in any form of manual labor and weren't directly involved in production of any kind; (2) the plebeians, or common people, were producers, farmers, and merchants; (3) the slaves, who were virtually bereft of rights. While the plebeians were free, they weren't afforded the same rights as their rulers. The patricians enjoyed *"otium,"* or leisure, while the fate of the plebeians was that of *"opus,"* or work.

In the 16th century, the term *"negoce"* was used to indicate a "discussion to reach an agreement." By the 17th century, the term took on a more commercial connotation. *"Faire le négoce de,"* for example (a term still used in French), means "to run a business, to trade." Eventually, *"negociation"* replaced *"negoce"* to mean "a discussion to reach an agreement."

The modern French word *"négociant"* (merchant, businessman) derives from *"négoce."* Wine merchants in Bordeaux are still called *"négociants"* (in the sense of bargainers), whereas *"négociateur"* is used to denote one skilled in the art of mediating important affairs, such as treaties or contracts.

Many definitions have been offered for negotiation across the years. For our purpose, negotiation should be defined as the act of ironing out differences through discussion between two or more parties in order to reach a satisfactory compromise involving an exchange of services or commodities. What is at stake may be tangible (cash or goods) or intangible (time or information).

Negotiation is a uniquely human ability. Adam Smith, in *The Wealth of Nations*, rightfully wrote, *"Nobody ever saw a dog make a fair and deliberate exchange of one bone for another with another dog."*[10] We've developed much more sophisticated methods of allocating resources than animals have. Civilizations have emerged thanks in part to our aptitude in trade and bargaining. In order to protect us from ourselves and ensure the peaceful enjoyment of property, the rule of law has put limits on what, when, and how negotiation takes place.

[1] Cutting the Cake

A compromise is the art of dividing a cake in such a way that everyone believes he has the biggest piece.

Ludwig Erhard[11]

When we negotiate, our dilemma is that we must cooperate to avoid (or solve) a conflict, while at the same time competing for gains. We need to accept to move from a competitive position to a cooperative one. The more

---

[10] Adam Smith, *The Wealth of Nations*, ed. Laurence Dickey (Indianapolis: Hackett Classics, 1993), 11.

[11] This quote is generally attributed to Ludwig Erhard, German politician and second chancellor of the Federal Republic of Germany.

competitive we are, the harder it will be to reach an agreement. All negotiators come to the table with an implicit agreement that the cake is going to be cut. It is their challenge to determine how best to divide it.

If you have no intention, as a negotiator, to share anything valuable with the other party, you limit your chances of a successful outcome. It seems obvious that negotiation is a trade, yet many believe a sleight of hand will affect the outcome in their favor and forget this basic rule. John F. Kennedy had a clear understanding of this. In 1961, faced with the Berlin Crisis when the USSR demanded that all Allied forces be withdrawn from Berlin, Kennedy addressed his nation, informing Americans (and Russians) that B-52 and B-47 bombers were on alert, and famously said, *"We cannot negotiate with those who say, 'What's mine is mine, and what's yours is negotiable.'"*[12]

Obviously, the purpose of negotiation is to obtain a beneficial outcome. This could be to increase or maintain gains, power, or position (a party could seek a spot at the negotiating table to reduce its losses or preserve privileges that it feels are threatened). In all these cases, both parties believe that they will be better off if they reach an agreement. For this to be accomplished, a sequence of proposals and counterproposals is usually put forth until an agreement satisfactory to both parties is reached.

Creativity is an essential part of negotiation. Innovative means are necessary to find common ground and obtain personal benefit. The cake does not have to be equally shared, as there can be an imbalance of power in the negotiation, but a good deal will be one that satisfies both parties.

The more resources a person has available, the more inclined such person will be to negotiate. Scarcity of things leads to a limitation of exchange and an increase in competition. Burgundy wines and Bordeaux wines are some of the most sought-after wines in the world, but it is generally easier to buy Bordeaux wines produced in larger quantities than Burgundy wines, which are often limited to a few hundred bottles.

---

[12] "JFK Speech on Berlin" (President Kennedy speaks on the Berlin crisis. July 25, 1961) YouTube video, 31:37, "The Central Intelligence Agency." October 26, 2012. https://www.youtube.com/watch?v=c3Ww81yGLGU.

[2] The Choice to Trust

> Trust is choosing to risk making something you value vulnerable to another person's actions.
>
> —Charles Feltman[13]

Negotiation is a choice. If one party is forced to come to the table, this is an act of coercion, not a negotiation. Perhaps negotiation is imperative – it could be a matter of life or death, for you and others – but, in order for negotiation to take place, there has to be a voluntary relationship between all parties. Each of us decides what's under discussion, and how long this discussion will take place. Nonetheless, there can be an imbalance of power. When we discuss leverage, we'll address this imbalance in more detail.

While negotiation is a choice, it's anything but natural. Our instinctual response when we're faced with a threat is to flee, freeze, or fight. This is, of course, understandable: for many millennia, a quick, emotional reaction meant the difference between survival and death. Though threats are different in the modern world, our brains and bodies still react to our biological survival impulses. Successful negotiation requires us to overcome these hard-wired responses. It's easy to be taken by fear or anger, but discipline is required to understand and keep these natural impulses in check.

For any reasonable agreement to be reached, some degree of trust must exist between negotiating parties. It's rare for two people who've never met to begin their relationship on a foundation of trust. Every day, I see negotiators pitching sales without taking the time or effort to first build rapport. Trust must be earned; it's rarely immediate. Today, unprecedented competition for our attention has made us even more cautious. We must sound trustworthy

---

[13] Charles Feltman, *The Thin Book of Trust: An Essential Primer for Building Trust at Work* (Bend: Thin Book Publishing, 2009), 7.

and inspire confidence. Trust can come from a display of good and genuine intentions, a good track record, a referral, bonding, a patient attitude, the keeping of a promise, or small gestures such as offering help in an unrelated matter. While trust takes time to build, it can be lost in an instant.

Russian President Vladimir Putin once famously triggered a sense of distrust in German Chancellor Angela Merkel. Merkel, reportedly afraid of dogs, was less than pleased when Putin brought his hulking Labrador, Konni, to a meeting between the two leaders. In a photograph of the encounter, Merkel can be seen with her hand gripping the armrest of her chair, leaning away from the animal. Her face is pale, her eyes trained, with what looks like fear, on the beast. Putin's posture, on the other hand, is relaxed, his face widening into a smirk.

Brené Brown, a research professor at the University of Houston, has spent many years studying courage, vulnerability, shame, empathy, and trust. She's distilled what she's learned about how to gain the trust of another party into a simple acronym, BRAVING, which means:

Boundaries: There should be clear boundaries on both sides, to which all parties hold.
Reliability: We should consistently do what we say we're going to do.
Accountability: We should acknowledge, apologize for, and take accountability for the mistakes that we make.
Vault: We should hold the things that we share with one another in confidence.
Integrity: We should have good values.
Nonjudgment: If the other party is struggling, we shouldn't respond with judgment.
Generosity: In the context of negotiations, this could take the form of a gesture, patience, listening, or empathy.[14]

---

[14] Brene Brown, "The Power of Vulnerability," TEDx Houston, June 2010, 20:04, https://www.ted.com/talks/brene_brown_on_vulnerability/.

I think Brown's work is a great start, but I'd add the need for a negotiator not to appear defensive or aggressive (including not being passive-aggressive). Such attitudes can destroy trust. Your body language should harmonize with your words to avoid suspicion or reservation from the other party.

[3] Gaining Leverage

> It is far more lucrative and fun to leverage your strengths instead of attempting to fix all the chinks in your armor.
>
> —Timothy Ferriss[15]

One way to achieve successful negotiation is to improve a position through leverage. Leverage is possessing something the other party wants or the ability to create an outcome that they want to avoid at all costs. Leverage is power, and it takes many forms: status, knowledge, information, even threats (although negotiating under threat is not negotiating, as mentioned earlier). Power isn't about how hard you can hit; it's about striking true.

Great negotiators can be recognized by their ability to obtain successful outcomes with little leverage or their ability to find some as a discussion proceeds. You should be well aware of the value you can bring to the table and what the other party is seeking before negotiation begins.

Brexit is an excellent example of the scramble for leverage in a crucial negotiation. For the United Kingdom, Brexit has been one of the most complicated negotiations in its history. Existing agreements with other members of the European Union must be unraveled, and new ones must be forged. A complex chain link was built among all members in 45 years of integration. By any standard, Brexit is a political nightmare, one which will certainly benefit the lawyers lucky enough to gain a seat at the negotiating table.

---

[15] Timothy Ferriss, *The 4-Hour Workweek* (New York: Crown Archetype, 2010), 34.

Caught by surprise, the United Kingdom has been in a situation where its trade benefits with the European Union can be lost. The consequences may well be devastating as British goods and services may become less competitive as a result of higher tariffs imposed on them. Corporations established in the UK might move elsewhere to obtain the benefits of the EU market. Some products, such as medicine, may become difficult to find. The challenge for the British prime minister is to avoid a hard landing. Theresa May admitted early on[16] that she had limited leverage in the matter, and her abilities as a negotiator were certainly being tested.

In 2003, Marvin Kalb, from the Harvard University School of Government, interviewed Henry Kissinger.[17] The noted statesman recalled an anecdote from the Yom Kippur War, a conflict fought by a coalition of Arab states, led by Egypt and Syria, against Israel from October 6th through the 25th of 1973. The Soviet Union supported the Arab states, and the US supported Israel.

The Israelis were winning, and Leonid Brezhnev asked Kissinger, who was the US secretary of state at the time, to come to Moscow to discuss a ceasefire. Kissinger, an expert negotiator, elected to buy as much time as he could so Israel could continue improving its position, giving Kissinger increased bargaining power with the Russians and the Arab states.

When Kissinger arrived in Moscow, Brezhnev insisted on meeting the secretary in the Kremlin that very night. The Soviet leader demanded that a solution be reached, at the latest, by the following day. Kissinger told him that it wasn't within his power to authorize a solution. He was, after all, only secretary of state, and any binding agreement would require the approval of President Nixon. It is here that Brezhnev gained the upper hand. The Soviet leader informed Kissinger that there was no need to check with Nixon, as Nixon had sent a telegram granting Kissinger full authority to negotiate.

---

[16] Sir Malcolm Rifkind, "May Recognises limited leverage on Brexit talks," *Financial Times*, October 4, 2016.

[17] "How to Deal with a Crisis: Henry Kissinger on Negotiation Skills, Tactics (2003)," YouTube video, 59:32, "The Film Archives." March 26, 2016. https://youtu.be/oR1qUAHlndE/.

When he returned to the United States, Kissinger was furious. He had lost leverage and an opportunity to shape a better deal for the US. *"It was uncharacteristic,"* he said, *"of me to complain about having too much power."*

[4] The Search for a Fair Deal

> I try to be fair. When you do fair deals, both parties may not be 100 percent happy but you feel good about it and you tend to do more business over time and have more networking connections.
>
> —Mark Cuban[18]

Negotiation is often perceived in win-lose terms. This is a mistake, but it's also a natural impulse. In the fast-paced, sometimes-cutthroat world of business, the desire to win can shape our lives. The "winners" are those who rise to meet the greatest challenges. They are rewarded if not glorified.

When we're perceived as winners, it improves our social status, opens doors of opportunity, and often betters our financial situation. It makes you look good, but it can also make you feel good. Testosterone and dopamine levels are elevated in those who perceive themselves as winners (dopamine is an organic chemical and neurotransmitter that mediates reward and pleasure and is also linked to motivation and focus). Moreover, the accumulation of successes apparently changes the structure of our brain, making us smarter and more confident. Ian Robertson, professor of psychology at Trinity College, Dublin, developed this theory in his book *The Winner Effect* and considers that *"success is the greatest changer of the brain that mankind has ever known."*[19]

---

[18] Amy Jo Martin, Interview with Mark Cuban, *Why Not Now?*, episode 1, podcast audio, 2017, https://soundcloud.com/amyjomartin/.

[19] Ian Robertson, "Perfect Cities? The Winner Effect," TEDxDublin, 17:07, Oct 5, 2012, http://www.tedxdublin.com/portfolio-item/perfect-cities-the-winner-effect-ian-robertson-at-tedxdublin/.

We also live in a highly competitive world. Society encourages us to be smarter, to improve, and to strive for new heights. People come to cities in search of fortune. No wonder they tend to see negotiation as a competitive exercise.

America, for example, is considered to have a culture of "winning." The American language is replete with war and sports metaphors. If you're engaged in a high-risk venture that isn't likely to pay off, you're taking "a long shot." If you have a decided advantage, you're said to be "ahead of the game." If you achieve something no one in your peer group has, you've "raised the bar." You "make a killing," if you see a high rate of return, etc. This isn't to say that all Americans are affected by win-lose syndrome. Many great American negotiators see the value in an agreement that benefits all parties fairly, but the culture often tends to support a win-lose approach.

The win-lose syndrome is perhaps best articulated by Donald Trump. During his campaign announcement, he said, *"Our country is in serious trouble. We don't have victories anymore. We used to have victories, but we don't have them. When was the last time anybody saw us beating, let's say, China in a trade deal? They kill us. I beat China all the time. All the time. When did we beat Japan at anything? They send their cars over by the millions, and what do we do? When was the last time you saw a Chevrolet in Tokyo? It doesn't exist, folks. They beat us all the time."*[20]

Whoever feels this way sees negotiation as a zero-sum game. If you come to the table with this attitude, it can bring a negative and enduring effect on the way you interact with the other party. If you walk in with winning as your primary goal, you might assume you have nothing to lose by disadvantaging those with whom you're negotiating. Naturally, this perspective will reduce the chances that you'll build a worthwhile relationship, and it may increase your likelihood of affecting your (or your organization's) reputation. Such an attitude or reputation may make the other party justifiably cautious and less open to your ideas.

---

[20] "Donald Trump announces a presidential bid," *The Washington Post*, June 16, 2015.

A win-lose syndrome affecting both parties can lead to lose-lose outcomes. The most obvious causes of this are stubbornness, self-service bias, egocentrism, or appetite for money or status.

When we're in a win-lose state of mind, we're not in the best position to identify opportunities and make valuable exchanges with the other party. We abandon a great part of our creativity, an indispensable skill for any master negotiator. It is sometimes prudent to desert a position that can make quick cash if it can be detrimental in the long term. Quick money makers do not necessarily make good negotiators.

There is a category of negotiators who live in this state of mind and equate negotiation to a poker game. But negotiation isn't poker. Poker is about deception, but negotiation is about trust. Poker is about winning. Negotiation is about compromising. Having said this, some skills that benefit poker players, like an understanding of body language, carry over to negotiation.

By obtaining an unfair advantage, a negotiator runs the risk of seeing their deal dissolve in short order, or, even worse, turn an ally into an enemy. If the imbalance is too great, the underserved party may feel frustrated, even played, and will take any opportunity to leave this uncomfortable position.

I've seen this happen in the hotel business. It can occur when a hotel owner signs a management agreement for its property to the great benefit of a shameless hotel operator. In such cases, owners become understandably less cooperative with the operator during the term of the contract, waiting to renegotiate or to exit it, and creating tension for the hotel business. If these owners are well established in a country where the judicial system can't be fully trusted, then the situation can quickly become complicated for the operator.

In order to obtain fair deals, each party must strive to build bridges instead of fences. The more fairly these parties treat one another during this process, the better their chances of sharing a perspective, and reaching a common goal. A fair deal doesn't mean that parties will share all benefits and obligations equally. Rather, a fair deal is one by which both parties obtain a positive outcome.

John D. Rockefeller, legendary oil magnate, is still considered the wealthiest American in history. He had a reputation for being cutthroat, but this assessment was not always true. In many cases Rockefeller could have crushed a smaller business but instead gave its owners a hand so that both he and they could benefit. Rockefeller had all the power, but he also understood the benefits of compromise. A good example of this approach would be the situation of American railroads, which played a key role in the transport of refined oil produced by Rockefeller's refineries in the 19th century. By the dawn of the 20th century, however, these railroads were hardly competing against one another, and all struggling financially. Rather than hastening their fall, Rockefeller entered into an agreement in which the railroads could substantially increase their public prices, but had, in return, to grant rebates on the transfer of his oil. As their most valuable customer, then Rockefeller had tremendous leverage over competing refineries, which worried about future transport costs.[21]

While you should always try to negotiate the best terms possible for yourself, you shouldn't think in win-lose terms when doing it. This is true even for one-off transactions. In any negotiation, the minimum benefit is that everyone feels like they've been given a fair deal. As a "winner," you may face some sort of retaliation if this minimum isn't met – your reputation may be affected, and future opportunities could be lost.

---

[21] Ron Chernow, *Titan: The Life of John D. Rockefeller, Sr.* (New York: Vintage Books, 1998), 136.

[5] The Best Negotiators

> The reward of great men is that, long after they have died, one is not quite sure that they are dead.
>
> —Jules Renard[22]

History is full of talented negotiators. When we study the way that Churchill, Mandela, Talleyrand, Kissinger, and many others succeeded in negotiating deals – often against great odds, and often with hostile parties – we can draw real inspiration and learn how to better practice the craft. But we cannot compare these great negotiators directly. They all lived in different times and places, and their actions (and their skill in negotiating) evolved to meet the needs of the environments in which they lived. Each one had different challenges to confront and faced different people on the opposite side of their tables.

We sometimes see articles with titles like "Negotiate Like Churchill." While it may get clicks and attract readers, this doesn't make much sense. His determination, charisma, charm, and sense of humor should certainly be praised, and they were major factors in his success as a negotiator. Yet, behaving like Churchill is no guarantee of success today. We're not taking context into account. Moreover, authenticity is essential to negotiation. If the other party perceives that you're behaving in an affected manner, it is likely to damage their trust.

Having said this, great negotiators have some characteristics in common. Each has character and charisma. These are people who can command a room through their very presence. This enables them to build relationships and expand their influence in ways few others could. They have a deep understanding of human nature. They can spot the strengths and weaknesses in others and in themselves. It's not that these individuals are perfect – on the

---

[22] Jules Renard, *The Journal of Jules Renard* (New York: Tin House Books, 2008), 65.

contrary, it was their attitude toward their flaws, their determination to struggle with and overcome them, that distinguished such persons.

Great negotiators are willing to improve. They didn't start out as experts in negotiation (Churchill's life is full of failures in this respect), but they each remain focused and smartly persistent. They quickly bounce back when things don't work out. They are resilient. They are creative and adaptable.

Each of them knows how to access the right information, exercise patience, and surround themselves with the right people to assist them. We often underestimate the role played by teams surrounding great negotiators. Negotiation is rarely a solo exercise. Shadow men are often key to their preparation and success.

Among the great negotiators, to me, one has the total package. Charles Maurice de Talleyrand-Périgord (1754-1838) was a French statesman, diplomat, and one of the finest negotiators France has ever known. He was a mastermind – quick on the draw, able to thwart plots, influence the wiliest minds, and build a remarkable network of informants and allies. During the time that he lived and worked, France suffered great turmoil, and Talleyrand-Périgord worked to save as much of his nation as he could. This is nowhere clearer than after Napoleon's defeat in 1815, when France was at risk of being stripped by Russia, Austria, England, and Prussia.

Talleyrand-Périgord survived some of France's most turbulent decades, navigating the treacherous political waters of the Revolutionary, Napoleonic, and Bourbon Restoration regimes, and even becoming ambassador to the United Kingdom after the July Revolution of 1830. While, for over half a century, France had no lasting and reliable government, Talleyrand-Périgord contributed to keep the integrity of France's territory, remained alive, and retained his assets intact. Louis XVIII, the first monarch of the Bourbon Restoration, once asked him, *"I admire your influence on all what happened in France. How were you able to get rid of the Directoire and the omnipotence of Bonaparte?"*

The great statesman replied, *"Sire, I assure your Majesty that this is not my doing, something in me brings misfortune to governments that neglect me."*[23]

Talleyrand-Périgord had a peculiar way of working at a time when only the most rudimentary means of communication were available. He decided very quickly that, instead of drowning himself in paperwork, he'd be much more efficient if he delegated others to do this work for him. He had to find reliable and faithful people for it. He was always precise with his instructions, treated his employees respectfully, and rewarded them when they performed. These workers were very efficient and contributed greatly to his success as a master negotiator.

Talleyrand-Périgord had plenty of time to spend in salons, dinners, and elsewhere to gather precious information firsthand. He was also known to organize splendid events in Paris, attended by the most influential people. His mastery of the art of preparation kept him well informed. He was never rushing or overdoing things while negotiating. Talleyrand-Périgord knew that, with Europe in a state of constant conflict, it was unwise to make moves too quickly. He was more of a listener than a talker, and his words were all very well-chosen.[24] Far from being a perfect man (he was manipulative in many instances), his remarkable achievements now speak for themselves.

It's been said that the best negotiators can sell anything, or that they can obtain rights or benefits with nothing to offer in exchange. This type of negotiator often makes promises (such as future gains) or depict a suitable image to gain the other party's confidence. Whether they can keep these promises is another story. Another category will try to compensate for their lack of trustworthiness through displays of power and wealth. They remain influential only as long as they stay at the top, but winds can quickly change, and their influence easily collapses.

Great negotiators are like navigators. They are intuitive and adaptive and can react with equal skill to good fortune and adversity. They build their

---

[23] Louis Bastide, *Vie religieuse et politique de Talleyrand-Périgord: Prince de Bénévent* (Paris: Faure et Compagnie Editeurs, 1838), 348.

[24] Jules Bertaut, "Comment travaillait Talleyrand," *Le Monde Diplomatique*, October 1955.

reputation on their actual skills and their word is trusted because they value their own integrity above all else. These are not attributes that can be bought and worn like an expensive suit. They are elements of character that are honed through dedication and practice.

⌈IN ESSENCE⌋

- The more competitive you are, the more difficult negotiation will be for you. If you want to reach an agreement, move from a competitive mindset to a cooperative one.
- Make sure you have something of value to share with the other party before entering negotiation.
- Look for a fair deal, the one by which both parties obtain a positive outcome. Negotiation is not a win-lose game. This approach can damage your chances of a successful outcome, hurt your reputation, and limit future opportunities.
- Play the long-term game for better business and connections. Quick money makers do not necessarily make good negotiators.
- Trust is an essential precondition to negotiation. Establish it as early as possible. Inspire confidence and behave consistently and reliably. Don't be aggressive.
- Leverage is power in negotiation. Find the right leverage to use at the right time. Power is not about how hard you can hit but about striking true.
- The best negotiators are like navigators. They are intuitive and adaptive and can react with equal skill to good fortune and adversity.
- Build bridges and not fences.

CHAPTER TWO:

The Art of Preparation

Anticipation is the ultimate power. Losers react; leaders anticipate.

—Tony Robbins[25]

A good negotiator must be a master of anticipation and preparation. Preparation plays a key role in negotiation and is certainly not limited to knowing well the subject matter of a discussion. Your expertise or the quality of your product may not be enough to lead you to success. Collecting valuable information is key. Your mind and body must assemble and work in harmony toward the objective. Your attitude, style, and approach of negotiation have an important impact on the outcome.

In Japanese culture, laying groundwork is understood to be an essential element of the decision-making process. The concept, called *"nemawashi,"* literally means "wrap the roots." Imagine you must move a tree. In order to do so without killing the plant, it's essential to dig around the roots and wrap them. For the Japanese, this concept is thoroughly applied to the business world. To establish influence, people must work upstream, gain trust, and come to a consensus with those in power before any negotiation formally takes place. We can all learn from the concept of *nemawashi*.

---

[25] Tony Robbins, *Money: Master the Game—7 Simple Steps to Financial Freedom* (New York: Simon & Schuster, 2014), 30.

⌈6⌋ Gather Useful Data

It is a capital mistake to theorise before one has data.

—Sir Arthur Conan Doyle[26]

Before you sit across from a counterpart at a meeting, you must do your very best beforehand to understand the other party's interests, needs, objectives, strengths, weaknesses, situation, factors, and so forth. This exercise requires the display of actionable intelligence. With more data surrounding us, the ability to collect it and analyze it is an absolute critical skill for a negotiator.

Madeleine Albright, former United States secretary of state, in an interview with *The Harvard Gazette*,[27] gave a tasteful example of how small preparation details can be significant. Albright negotiated with former Syrian President Hafez al-Assad when she was in office. She had been warned by her predecessors of Assad's use of "bladder diplomacy." He would constantly offer tea and lemonade during negotiations to create a need to go to the bathroom and a discomfort, hoping the other party would rush into things. Albright politely declined any beverage, she said, and won that small battle.

As in international relations, collecting valuable information is indispensable to succeed in the business world. You determine what you do with what you know. The quality of the information you gather affects the clearness of your sight.

For many established businesses, a host of public information is now available. Sometimes, it is willingly made public (such as data released by listed companies) or finds its way into the public sphere through leaks from employees, suppliers, advisors, or more. If the other party did its homework

---

[26] Sir Arthur Conan Doyle, *The Adventures of Sherlock Holmes*, "A Scandal in Bohemia" (New York: Harper & Brothers, 1892), 7.

[27] Robert O'Neill, "Albright, on negotiating," *The Harvard Gazette*, April 3, 2015.

on you or your business, neglecting to do yours will leave you at a disadvantage. You'll have less knowledge and less leverage than a well-prepared counterpart. If you're not minimally aware of the other party's recent deals, products, services, management, and so on, you're bound to make some incorrect assumptions or miss opportunities.

Sam Walton, founder of Wal-Mart, was a master at gathering information. In his autobiography, *Made in America*, we learn that he always brought a legal pad and tape recorder with him. Walton wasn't comfortable doing his work cramped up in an office behind the same desk every day. Sociable and charming, Walton would frequently engage strangers (including customers) in conversation. He always paid close attention to his competition, visiting their stores or sending scouts to gain insight into what made others in his field successful. He began using private planes in the 1960s, the first retailer in the US to do so. Before he would develop a supermarket in an area, he would fly to the target, look at how the town was growing, and learn all he could about local competition. In a highly competitive sector, Walton was consistently ahead of trends. When he sat at the negotiation table, he knew it all. Even outside of work, when he was dining or playing tennis with someone, he'd done his homework.

Emphasis should also be put on the individuals with whom you'll be dealing. You should try to learn about their personality, interests, and behaviors. This knowledge will help you understand how to best approach them, trigger their emotions, or predict their moves. Social media, memberships, event attendance, and more can help you to gain insight to their preferences, habits, and networks. Your research may even illuminate common grounds. The more you have in common with someone, the more that person will find you sympathetic and relatable.

Whenever possible, double-check the information you've gathered. The Internet is full of nonsense and misinformation. Vigilance is key to ensure that research is reliable and from credible sources. The same cautiousness applies to word of mouth or whistle blowers.

With new technologies generating a barrage of data, it can be overwhelming to swim in an ocean of information and a challenge for negotiators to identify valuable intelligence to be used as leverage. You need to find the right shortcuts, connect the right dots, use the right tools, and tally the collected information. Although convenient, the Internet should not be your only source. Well-related gatherings, meetings, receptions, dinners, and conferences offer good opportunities to gather useful information.

Gathering data also means knowing the subject matter of your discussions with others. You must be knowledgeable about the topics upon which you are negotiating and leave no stone unturned.

Mark Cuban became a reputable negotiator (and a billionaire) by applying the above principles. When asked by a young entrepreneur how he managed to be ahead of the game, he said: *"Someone is out there looking to put you out of business. Someone is out there who thinks they have a better idea than you have. A better solution than you have. A better or more efficient product than you have. If there is someone out there who can 'kick your ass' by doing it better, it's part of your job as the owner of the company to stay ahead of them and 'kick your own ass' before someone else does."*[28]

It's the plain truth. If you want to optimize your negotiations, start by knowing your own business inside and out. As you collect and learn valuable information, that information becomes knowledge, and this accrued knowledge can translate into negotiating power.

---

[28] "Mark Cuban: Best Interview UNCENSORED," YouTube Video, 57:42, "Valuetainment." November 23, 2015, https://www.youtube.com/watch?v=S8yjzUqK1zQ/.

[7] Your Attitude Makes a Big Difference

> It isn't our position, but our disposition that makes us happy. Remember, some people freeze in the winter. Others ski. A positive attitude always creates positive results. Attitude is a little thing that makes a big difference.
>
> —John Mason[29]

Your preconceived ideas of how a negotiation is going to play out will influence its outcome and your relationship with the parties involved. Your attitude toward negotiation contains three important elements: energy level, confidence, and motivation. For instance, if a negotiation is perceived as a win-lose game (motivation), your discussion may quickly become adversarial and the outcome will likely be poor. If negotiation is attended half-heartedly (energy level), there's a good chance that creativity will be stifled.

Successful negotiation requires positive energy and the creation of an environment that encourages cooperation. The attitude with which you enter a negotiation and the energy you diffuse plays a determinant role in that negotiation's success. Positive energy increases your level of confidence and your capacity to absorb stress, makes you more influential, and opens your mind.

Before negotiation starts, your body and mind should be brought into a state of positivity. This state should be maintained to the highest possible extent throughout negotiation. Many factors can prevent you from reaching this optimum state: your physiology, distractions (such as a new message flashing on your phone), the setting in which the negotiation takes place, what you ate before a meeting, and more. Make sure you're in control of these factors before negotiating. We will develop them further in this book.

---

[29] John Mason, *Know Your Limits* (Tulsa, Oklahoma: Insight Publishing Group, 1999), 41.

Few people know that the human brain and heart work in tandem to generate a powerful energy field. They also work together with the endocrine system in reaction to external and internal stimuli through emotional responses. The electromagnetic amplitude of the heart muscle is 60 times more significant than that of the human brain. The heart produces the strongest electromagnetic field in the human body. Your biochemistry literally produces electricity. *"The heart is a pump that does respond when the brain asks it to, but it is not enslaved to the brain. Its relationship to the brain is more like a marriage with each dependent on the other. It seems science is now restoring to the heart something that rightfully belongs to it: our emotions,"* says David Malone, science filmmaker and producer of *Heart vs Mind: What Makes Us Human*.[30]

The intensity and type of emotions we experience affect the electromagnetic signals and behavioral cues that eventually reach other people. Recent research suggests that *"the heart's electromagnetic field decreases in electrical coherence as an individual becomes angry or frustrated and increases in coherence as a person shifts to such positive emotional states as sincere love, care or appreciation."*[31] Magnetic attractions and repulsions occur through the biochemistry of our emotional state, so it is crucial to have your heart in the right place when you enter negotiations.

A negotiator will generally make fewer mistakes when their mind is positively charged, and they feel empowered. Negativity narrows their focus and tends to aim it in the wrong direction (often at themselves).

A great way to trigger positivity is by resetting your physiology. Check your posture, open your chest, and make sure that your breathing is deep and calm. Wear a smile on your face and practice a sense of presence. Try not to enter meetings (or even begin a conference call) slouching, squinting, or

---

[30] David Malone, *Hearts vs Minds*, (UK, BBC, 2012), https://www.bbc.co.uk/programmes/b01kpvj1).

[31] Rollin McCraty, PhD, Mike Atkinson, Dana Tomasino, BA, and William A. Tiller, "The Electricity of Touch: Detection and measurement of cardiac energy exchange between people" (The HeartMath Institute, Boulder, California, 1998).

sighing. Your body has a great influence on your mind – this is what scientist call "embodied cognition."[32] Your physical state can generate a positive or negative response in your mind. Smiling, for example, has been proven to trigger positive emotions. Laughter, too.

Amy Cuddy, a social psychologist at Harvard Business School, has demonstrated that simple changes in posture can increase testosterone and decrease cortisol levels. The way you sit or stand can give you more confidence to endure a challenging and stressful negotiation. According to Cuddy, good posture can make you feel in control, unthreatened, and safe. You can pose like a cowboy or a model, or even put your feet on the desk to feel more powerful when preparing for negotiation. Power postures during negotiation should be subtler. Your legs should remain uncrossed and with both feet on the ground, avoid touching your face, open your chest and shoulders, and appear relaxed and confident.

Displaying a power posture shouldn't have anything to do with intimidation. The objective is to increase your personal level of confidence not to intimidate. If your confidence is not showing, perceptive parties will be able to see the cracks in your façade and exploit your weaknesses. If you are confident (and you should be), you will appear confident.

Confidence is not arrogance or stubbornness either. A stubborn or arrogant negotiating style has been shown to be comparatively ineffective. A study carried out by Andrea Kupfer Schneider on a group of lawyers showed that their effectiveness in negotiation drops substantially if they position themselves as adversarial and stubborn.[33] However, when they show empathy and appear to be problem solvers, they are more persuasive and more likely to arrive at a fair deal.

Confidence isn't showing that you know it all; it's being prepared to answer any question pertinent to the negotiation with no fear or discomfort.

---

[32] Samuel McNerney, "A Brief Guide to Embodied Cognition: Why You Are Not Your Brain," *Scientific American* Guest Blog, November 4, 2011.

[33] Andrea Kupfer Schneider, "Shattering Negotiation Myths: Empirical Evidence on the Effectiveness of Negotiation Style," *Harvard Negotiation Law Review*, 143, (2002).

Once your energy and confidence level have been raised, ask yourself what the higher purpose of the negotiation is. Is money your primary motivation? When corporations and their leaders implement a system of rewards and punishments, it can sometimes narrow the minds of their workers and trigger unethical behaviors.[34] An organization which is strongly driven by a paradigm of rewards and punishments can generate narrow-minded negotiators, more concerned with earning bonuses (or avoiding punishment) than with brokering the best deals. If you're trained to think of your job as a negotiator in pecuniary terms, then making money will be your obsession. Incentives can be effective but have limits that corporations should be aware of. Dan Ariely, professor of psychology and behavioral economics at Duke University, among others, found that large stakes can lead to big mistakes:

> *Psychological research suggests that excessive rewards can in some cases produce supra-optimal motivation, resulting in a decline in performance. To test whether very high monetary rewards can decrease performance, we conducted a set of experiments at MIT, the University of Chicago, and rural India. Subjects in our experiment worked on different tasks and received performance-contingent payments that varied in amount from small to large relative to their typical levels of pay. With some important exceptions, we observed that high reward levels can have detrimental effects on performance.*[35]

The 2008 financial crisis is a powerful example of how people can be blinded by greed. This was caused when banks bundled together mortgages to form a financial instrument called mortgage-backed securities. They were seen as a low-risk investment because they were backed by a default insurance. Banks demanded more mortgages from their base to support profitable sales of these instruments. Their employees were incentivized to sell mortgages to

---

[34] Dan Pink, "The Puzzle of Motivation," TED Global, July 2009, 18:25, https://www.ted.com/talks/dan_pink_on_motivation/.

[35] Dan Ariely, Uri Gneezy, George Loewenstein, and Nina Mazar, "Large Stakes and Big Mistakes." *Review of Economic Studies* (2009), 76, 451-469.

people who sometimes couldn't afford them. Interest rates went up, defaults multiplied, housing prices fell with housing supply outpacing demand. Homeowners could neither repay the banks nor sell their houses. This created one of the biggest financial crises in human history.

The most valuable and lasting negotiators aren't primarily driven by bonuses or other flashy incentives. They first see themselves as problem solvers meant to create value for themselves and others.

⌈8⌋ Be Focused

You can't depend on your eyes when your imagination is out of focus.

—Mark Twain[36]

For negotiators, focus is key. It makes them more creative and productive. Negotiators have to be focused on what matters. So often, we can tell through body language that others aren't really listening, that they aren't there for the dialogue that's taking place. Perhaps the most egregious example of this is when people try to talk and text at once. The second you hold your phone (even if it's turned off), you send a signal to others that you are not fully with the people in the room.

Texts, emails, calls, alerts, and other distractions are inevitable in the workplace. Research shows that, on average, we are interrupted 87 times a day at work, and that it takes over 23 minutes to fully regain focus.[37,38] You don't need to read a scientific article to appreciate the truth of this. As Cal

---

[36] Mark Twain, *A Connecticut Yankee in King Arthur's Court* (New York: Harper & Brothers Publishers, 1889) 421.

[37] Jennifer Robinson. Interview with Gloria Mark, PhD, associate professor at the Donald Bren School of Information and Computer Sciences at the University of California, Irvine. Gallup Business Journal Online. June 8, 2006, https://news.gallup.com/businessjournal/23146/too-many-interruptions-work.aspx#1/.

[38] Terri Griffith. "Help Your Employees Find Flow," *Harvard Business Review*, April 17, 2014.

Newport, author and Georgetown University professor, puts it in his book *Deep Work*, "We have turned ourselves into human network routers with frequent breaks for quick hits of distraction."[39] We cannot produce quality work if we are constantly distracted. When we are unfocused, we're more likely to make mistakes.

Some corporations encourage multitasking, expecting their employees to be highly responsive with their emails, sometimes regardless of the other tasks they're engaged in. Remember the blinking red light on the Blackberry? I certainly do. I found it incredibly annoying, as if someone was tapping me on my shoulder every time I received an email, wherever I was. It seemed designed to keep me on my toes 24/7. The reality is that multitasking doesn't make us more productive. Michael John Harris, Canadian author and journalist, is right when he states that *"When we think we're multitasking we're actually multiswitching. That is what the brain is very good at doing – quickly diverting its attention from one place to the next. We think we're being productive. We are, indeed, being busy. But in reality, we're simply giving ourselves extra work."*[40]

Of course, the more available and responsive you are, the better you look to your employer. Often, managers judge themselves by this same standard. Busy business owners may see quick responsiveness as a sign that they are on top of things. This approach may look good on paper, but it can be toxic to negotiation. When we're preparing for a meeting, or when we're in it, we shouldn't overload our brains with unnecessary information. We must come to the table with the clearest ideas and the clearest mind. If locked for hours in a conference room and stakes are high, taking short breaks can help to improve focus. Don't spend these breaks checking unrelated emails or making non-urgent phone calls. Just clear your head, take some fresh air, and breathe.

My advice is to turn off your phone when you enter a meeting. The only reason to have your device turned on is if it has content you intend to share

---

[39] Cal Newport, *Deep Work: Rules for Focused Success in a Distracted World* (New York: Hachette, 2016), 6.

[40] Michael John Harris, *The End of Absence: Reclaiming What We've Lost in a World of Constant Connection* (New York: Penguin Group, 2014), 117.

during your discussions. The first minutes of a negotiation may be when your credibility is not yet established and most easily tested. You should be present. You can easily plan ahead and ensure you've set the time aside to negotiate with as little distraction as possible. The vast majority of calls, texts, and emails we receive don't require an immediate response.

With the emergence of modern electronic media including the Internet, tablets, mobile phones, smart watches, and so forth, our attention is more divided than ever. Brands and products are constantly competing for it. We carry our smartphones everywhere and many streams of information are fed to a single individual at a single time, causing a chokepoint in information uptake. We absorb a tremendous amount of data each day. By 2020, 1.7 MB of data will be created every second for every person on earth.[41] The communications industry is expected to consume 20 percent of all the world's electricity by 2025.[42,43] It is not a wave; it is a tsunami.

A barrage of data divides our focus. If your attention is frayed, spreading in all directions, you're going to be less effective as a negotiator. Our short-term memory becomes adversely affected by digital information.[44] We spend more time receiving and processing the information we're presented than we do using it.

The science of decision-making shows that the flow of information we receive every day affects the way that we think. An overload of data has been identified with certain negative thought patterns, among which are the failure to decide, the feeling of regret for forgone options, the preference for newer information only because it is new, and a lack of creativity.[45] The best way to

---

[41] "Data Never Sleeps," DOMO trade paper, https://www.domo.com/assets/downloads/18_domo_data-never-sleeps-6+verticals.pdf/.

[42] John Vidal, "'Tsunami of data' could consume one fifth of global electricity by 2025," *Climate Home News*, November 12, 2017.

[43] "'Tsunami of data' could consume one fifth of global electricity by 2025," *The Guardian*, December 11, 2017.

[44] David Callahan, "Online time can hobble brain's important work," KTH The Royal Institute of Technology, September 20, 2013.

[45] Sharon Begley, "The Science of Making Decisions," *Newsweek*, February 27, 2011.

circumvent data overload impact on your brain and behavior is to make a conscious decision to limit the excessive load of information in the first place.[46]

In 1716, humans hadn't yet experienced all the distractions that came with the electronic age. Even then, however, wise negotiators knew the importance of maintaining focus. François de Callières, author and diplomat, informed Philippe II, Duke of Orleans, *"that the necessary qualities of a negotiator are an observant mind, a spirit of application which refuses to be distracted by pleasures or frivolous amusements, a sound judgement which takes the measure of things as they are, and which goes straight to his goal by the shortest and most natural paths without wandering into useless refinements and subtleties which as a rule only succeed in repelling those with whom one is dealing."*[47] His words are even more true today.

Your focus, as a negotiator, is very much dependent on your sleep. The sharper your mind is, the better you'll perform. You have to stay alert so that you can detect cues, weigh up proposals efficiently, maintain self-awareness, and remain creative. Any experienced negotiator knows the fatigue that comes with involved negotiation and a heavy workload. Some negotiations can be truly intense, lasting for days, weeks, months, or even years. The neglect of sleep is an unfortunate symptom of the modern condition. We want to do more than we reasonably should in a 24-hour period. However, sleep is essential to memory consolidation. We need about 8 hours of sleep a night to integrate the day's experiences with our existing knowledge. Sleep is also crucial to maintain cognitive ability. Whatever time you gained by missing sleep comes at the price of diminished creativity and focus. Your judgment gets clouded while you become more easily aggressive and impatient.[48]

We often underestimate the benefits of napping and wrongly associate it with laziness. A power nap of 20 minutes every day improves your alertness and performance without leaving you dazed or affecting your nighttime

---

[46] Bernard Marr, "Why Too Much Data Is Stressing Us Out," *Forbes,* November 25, 2015.

[47] François de Callières, *On the Manner of Negotiating with Princes* (Paris: Mercure Galant, 1716), 18.

[48] Anne Field, "Why Sleep Is So Important," *Harvard Business Review,* January 14, 2009.

sleep. John D. Rockefeller and Winston Churchill, two of history's greatest negotiators, napped daily. Rockefeller went so far as to say, *"I know of nothing more despicable and pathetic than a man who devotes all the waking hours of the day to making money for money's sake [...] I attribute my good condition to my almost reckless independence in determining for myself what to do and the rigid adhering to regulations which give me the maximum of rest and quiet and leisure, and I am being richly paid for it every day."*[49]

Churchill said, *"Nature has not intended mankind to work from eight in the morning until midnight without that refreshment of blessed oblivion, which, even if it only lasts twenty minutes, is sufficient to renew all the vital forces."*[50]

As negotiators, we can learn a great deal from some studies carried out on how to reduce fatigue-related risks and improve the performance of air pilots, whose focus is of crucial importance. These studies tell us, for instance, that quality of sleep is as important as quantity, and sleep becomes more fragmented between the ages of 50 and 60. Additionally, caffeine makes it harder to fall asleep, and sleep at work is usually not as good as that at home.[51,52]

---

[49] Ron Chernow, *Titan: The Life of John D. Rockefeller, Sr.* (New York: Penguin Random House LLC, 1998), 122.

[50] Joseph Cardieri, "Churchill Understood Afternoon Naps," *The New York Times*, October 2, 1989.

[51] The International Federation of Air Line Pilots' Associations, *Fatigue Management Guide for Airline Operations. 2015 Edition.*

[52] Andreas Tittelbach, *Pilot Fatigue Barometer,* The European Cockpit Association, 2012.

[9] Learn to Discipline Your Mind

> If you don't take the time to think proactively you will increasingly find yourself reacting to your environment rather than influencing it.
>
> —Jeff Weiner[53]

An overload of information and distraction, uncontrolled emotions, and stress are just some of the factors that can prevent you from being centered. To achieve optimum results in negotiation, seek the best in yourself to influence and inspire others. Meditation is a great tool for mental discipline, and many world-class negotiators have discovered its virtues.

Most of the time, instead of controlling our minds, we allow our mind to control us. Let's be honest, our heads are more often in the past or the future than they are in the present. For negotiators, developing a sense of mindfulness can be tremendously beneficial.

In general, meditation can be defined as a practice of directing our focus to a single thing or to nothing in particular. In the second case, meditation involves letting thoughts come and go without judgment. When we meditate, we channel our thoughts, reset our minds, and increase our focus.

Many believe that the purpose of meditation is to generate a state of inner peace. As a practitioner, I feel that meditation is more about cultivating positive energy, which is essential in building meaningful relationships with others.

Meditation has a positive impact on our mood as it increases the experience we have of positive emotions. It prevents us from rushing to judgment, helps us hone our observational skills, and allows us to better cope with stress. In a study published in *The Journal of Personal Psychology*, an experiment was performed on working adults who were asked to begin a "practice of

---

[53] Jeff Weiner, LinkedIn CEO, "The Importance of Scheduling Nothing," LinkedIn Article, April 3, 2013.

loving-kindness and meditation." According to the results, this produced an increase in positive emotions, which expanded the practitioners' personal resources such as "increased mindfulness, purpose in life, social support," and decreased illness."[54] Long-term meditation actually changes the brain. The gray matter in areas known to moderate emotions, compassion, coordination, and memory grows.[55,56,57]

Meditation is also source of creativity. Open-monitoring meditation (monitoring of the present without judgment) is proven to stimulate divergent thinking and generate creative ideas.[58]

Ray Dalio, founder of Bridgewater Associates, the world's largest hedge fund firm, is a well-known advocate of meditation. His says, *"meditation leads to open-mindedness. To creativity. Meditating is a process of opening up. It's like taking a hot shower – even though you're not thinking of something, a great idea comes through and you just grab it."*[59]

Many successful and innovative leaders in today's business climate are aware of this helpful practice, and some make resources available for their employees. For instance, Google currently has a mindfulness program for its workers called "Search Inside Yourself." Apple, Nike, McKinsey & Co.,

---

[54] Barbara L. Fredrickson, Michael A. Cohn, Kimberly A. Coffey, Jolynn Pek, and Sandra M. Finkel, "Open Hearts Build Lives: Positive Emotions, Induced Through Loving-Kindness Meditation, Build Consequential Personal Resources," *Journal of Personal Social Psychology*, 2008, 95(5):1045-1062.

[55] Sara W. Lazar, Catherine E. Kerr, Rachel H. Wasserman, Jeremy R. Gray, Douglas N. Greve, Michael T. Treadway, Metta McGarvey, Brian T. Quinn, Jeffery A. Dusek, Herbert Benson, Scott L. Rauch, Christopher I. Moore, and Bruce Fischl. "Meditation experience is associated with increased cortical thickness." *Neuroreport*, 16(17), (2005), 1893–1897.

[56] Brigid Schulte. Interview with Sarah Lazar, neuroscientist at Massachusetts General Hospital and Harvard Medical School. The Washington Post Online. May 26, 2015.

[57] Harvard Medical School Longwood Seminars. "Now and Zen: How mindfulness can change your brain and improve your health." March 8, 2016, Boston, MA.

[58] Lorenza S. Colzato, Ayca Ozturk, and Bernhard Hommel, "Meditate to create: the impact of focused-attention and open-monitoring training on convergent and divergent thinking," *Frontiers in Psychology 2012;* 3:116.

[59] "Ray Dalio on Meditation (2004)" YouTube Video, 1:58, "Bhuwana Properti" March 12, 2014. https://youtu.be/zM-2hGA-k5E/.

and many others are known to offer quiet rooms and meditation courses to their employees. Jack Dorsey, CEO of Twitter, makes meditation part of his daily routine. He wakes up at 5:00 a.m. to meditate for half an hour.[60] John D. Rockefeller used to meditate and talk to himself.

Often, people miss out on the benefits of meditation because they do not understand that meditation is accessible to all. They neglect to practice it because they believe that it is too difficult, too ritualistic, or that only long sessions are effective. This isn't true. Meditating as little as ten minutes a day can improve your skills and have positive effects.

Personally, I find meditation in cold water especially powerful. When you're in cold water, you see more clearly and more quickly. I find it to be singularly effective in elevating consciousness. It is like opening a secret doorway to the soul. The heart starts beating faster, forcing the body to breathe efficiently and the mind to develop focus.

Before any kind of important meeting, a few minutes of meditation can reduce stress, increase your attention and energy, and heighten your level of awareness. Your sensory capacity is enhanced, and you're in a much better position to begin negotiation. If you're locked in a room for several hours, a wise idea is to take a break and engage in five minutes of breathing or mindfulness. This gift to yourself has been shown to be an effective way to reset your focus, improve your blood pressure, and relieve stress.

To help you with meditation, two exercises have been developed for readers of *The Master Key* in cooperation with Master Grace Kim. They can be downloaded for free on https://www.ludovic.online/meditation (password: imeditate).

Along with meditation, visualization techniques can be useful to negotiators as well. They also improve creativity, confidence, and focus. Visualization basically consists in mapping your mind through a repeated projection of images and positive energy. These are things you want to happen and you believe in. It's like working on a puzzle with the advantage of already

---

[60] "Jack Dorsey, live chat(2105)" ProductHunt.com "Jack Dorsey." December 22, 2015. https://www.producthunt.com/live/jack-dorsey/.

knowing how the puzzle will look like when completed.

When you enter a negotiation already having visualized where you want to go and how to get there, you get less distracted by events occurring during negotiation or in connection with it. Negotiators who spend time thinking about how the other side sees the problem are proven to generate more valuable outcomes for themselves.[61]

Visualization techniques are well-known by athletes to improve their performance. They pump themselves up with confidence, think about all possible ways to get there, and picture themselves holding the trophy. Imagery is proven to stimulate the human brain, activating part of the brain playing a key role in motor activation, and help it to map actions necessary to achieve set goals.[62]

The power of visualization cannot be better illustrated than with the story of Natan Sharansky, the ex-Soviet Union dissident. Before being accused of spying for the benefit of the Americans and sentenced to 13 years of forced labor in 1978, Sharansky used to play chess. He even won a championship in his native city of Donetsk at the age of 15. His dream was to become a chess champion one day. Deprived of a chess board in jail, Sharansky started playing games in his mind, developing tremendous abilities to anticipate chess moves. After being released, Sharansky moved to Israel. It happened that in 1996, he was among the 25 Israelis to take on Gary Kasparov, world chess champion, in a simultaneous chess exhibition. Sharansky beat Kasparov that night and said that he had little time for chess during his dissident years in the Soviet Union, but he recovered his skills in prison, where he said he spent the long days in solitary confinement playing three simultaneous games in his mind.[63]

---

[61] Adam D. Galinsky, William W. Maddux, Debra Gilin, and Judith B. White, "Why It Pays to Get Inside the Head of Your Opponent: The Differential Effects of Perspective Taking and Empathy in Negotiations," *Psychological Science,* 19, Issue 4 (April 2008), 378-384.

[62] Sébastien Hétu, Mathieu Gregoire, Arnaud Saimpont, Michel-Pierre Coll, Fanny Eugène, Pierre-Emmanuel Michon, and Philip Jackson, "The neural network of motor imagery: An ALE meta-analysis." *Neuroscience and Biobehavioral Review, 37 (2013) 930–949.*

[63] Serge Schmemann. "Kasparov Beaten in Israel, by Russians." *The New York Times.* October 16, 1996.

[10] Self-Awareness: A Vital Attribute

The truth about a man is in what he hides.

—André Malraux[64]

An aptitude for introspection is an indispensable tool for a master negotiator. Yet a clear and honest self-awareness is a rare quality to possess and act upon. Those who embody honest self-awareness, are usually humbler, which makes them more likable and authentic, and therefore more influential.

Negotiating with confidence but ignoring your weaknesses may work for a while, but when facing a master negotiator, one who can spot these weaknesses and use them to their advantage, you're likely to lose leverage. If you can't see the chinks in your armor, they may cost you dearly.

Leaders who develop self-awareness tend to be more efficient and successful. They listen, observe what is happening around them, accept constructive criticism, and grow.[65] Many studies show that when you are self-aware, you are more confident, a better communicator, more creative, and more emotionally intelligent.[66]

Alan Mulally, former Boeing executive and CEO of Ford Motor Company, employed self-awareness during his time in leadership. Under Mulally's guidance, Ford went from being a company in debt to a highly profitable one. In an interview given to Georgetown University in 2016, he explained that self-awareness plays an important role in successful leadership. Technical skills and an ability to strategize are important, but a self-aware person is better

---

[64] André Malraux, *Antimémoires* (Paris: Gallimard, 1967), 8.

[65] Rasmus Hougaard, Jacqueline Carter, and Marissa Afton, "Self-Awareness Can Help Leaders More Than an MBA Can," *Harvard Business Review*, January 12, 2018.

[66] Daniel Goleman, "Self-Awareness: The Foundation of Emotional Intelligence," LinkedIn Article, January 13, 2017.

prepared to effectively work with others.[67]

Two types of self-awareness are generally offered. The first is an introspection about ourselves including our qualities, flaws, thoughts, feelings, beliefs, motivations, and so on. The second form of self-awareness is knowing how we're perceived by others by soliciting feedback.

When you're self-aware, you act in a more constructive way. You're more receptive to others' ideas and are more able to identify the right decision and the right people in the right moment. This comes, in part, from an increased ability to see past your own ego.

With an egocentric mindset, outside ideas, regardless of their merit, may appear to be unworthy or even a threat. In addition, the more power you have, the more you tend to dismiss or reject others' points of view.

When it comes to accurately assessing our own capabilities, we're usually the least-qualified party. We tend to think we're more capable than we are and to rank ourselves higher than those of comparable ability, especially when we consider ourselves more experienced than them. Psychologist Tasha Eurich, interviewed by Wharton University on her book *Insight*, said, *"95% of people think they're self-aware, but the real number is closer to 10% to 15%. I always joke that on a good day, 80% of us are lying to ourselves about whether we're lying to ourselves. It can be problematic. A lot of times, the people who have the most room to improve are the least likely to know."*[68]

Self-awareness isn't easy. It's true that, in order to be self-aware, you have to be familiar with the workings of your conscious mind. You also need insight into your subconsciousness, which can be quite difficult to gain. Self-awareness requires you to take an impartial look at your own biases. Tasha Eurich suggests a way to avoid being trapped in negative and ruminating thoughts: instead of asking *why*, you should ask *what*. For instance, instead of asking *why* you couldn't convince people to buy your product, you should ask *what*

---

[67] "Alan Mulally on Leadership," Georgetown University, In Focus I Leadership Styles I Public Relations & Corporate Communications, YouTube Video, 8:20, "Georgetown SCS." November 1, 2016. https://www.youtube.com/watch?v=WXaFevYxgnY&feature=youtu.be/.

[68] "Are You a Self-Aware Leader?" Knowledge@Wharton, June 14, 2017.

you can do to be more convincing.[69]

Getting and listening to people's feedback is another form of self-awareness. Others' view of you is usually more accurate than your own. It should be done tactfully, in a way that doesn't make you seem indecisive or weak. If you ask people you trust in the right way, you'll be seen as wanting to get things right, to make the right adjustments so that you commit fewer errors or you don't repeat them. The person you ask may be wrong, but you should listen without judgment and analyze later.

Other simple ways of assessing your capabilities include recording important conversations you analyze later and paying greater attention to your peers' reaction when you speak.

Meditation is a good start on the way to becoming self-aware, since it allows you to experience the present and focus on the physical and psychological processes occurring within, creating a clean palate for thinking about your behaviors and understanding yourself.

Self-awareness requires thinking (if possible, far away from your smartphone). I hope one day you will have the chance to visit the Loire Valley in France. The beautiful city of Amboise is well-known for having been the last residence of Leonardo da Vinci. It is possible to visit his house (Le Clos Lucé) and see his great inventions. Some copies of his manuscripts are also offered to the public for viewing. I remember a quote from the inventor, extracted from one of them, and which has stuck in my mind. It said, *"The less you think, the more mistakes you make."*

---

[69] Tasha Eurich, "Increase your self-awareness with one simple fix," TedXMileHigh, November, 2017. https://www.ted.com/talks/tasha_eurich_increase_your_self_awareness_with_one_simple_fix?language=en/.

[11] First Impressions

The first impression is always the right one, especially when it is a bad one.

—Henri Jeanson[70]

First impressions are crucial. 80 percent of the information we receive is processed visually. According to Amy Cuddy,[71] there are two questions people ask themselves when they meet a new person: (1) *"Can I trust this person?"* and (2) *"Can I respect this person?"* The answer to both should be yes.

Trust is key in negotiation, and first impressions play an important role in gaining it. Unfortunately, the power of first impressions is often underestimated or neglected. Some people believe they are better off being their simplest self rather than worrying about the impression they make or believe that that judging someone at glance is inaccurate. These people should better understand human nature.

We humans can't analyze everything thoroughly all the time, therefore we tend to stereotype and take mental shortcuts. We've developed certain automatic responses that allow us to navigate situations in which we frequently find ourselves.

When you hear the word "Chinese," a series of associations might flash through your mind. You might think of tai chi, cheaply made products, crowded places, or crafty people. While this may be true of certain people or attributes of Chinese culture, such ideas are far from an all-encompassing picture of what the term "Chinese" means.

Suppose you have a meeting with a Chinese businessman. Your first impression will be affected by the stereotypes and biases you hold. Consciously

---

[70] Henri Jeanson, *Jeanson Par Jeanson* (Paris: René Chateau, 2000), 47. (French translation: "La première impression est toujours la bonne, surtout quand elle est mauvaise.")

[71] Amy Cuddy, *Presence* (New York: Little Brown and Company, 2015), 71.

or unconsciously, you'll look for evidence to confirm the assumptions you already have.

The concept of "thin slices" developed by social psychologists Nalini Ambady and Robert Rosenthal helps us understand how first impressions work and why they matter. Both psychologists showed that a small amount of visual information (such as body language and facial expressions) can be quickly analyzed to form accurate snap judgments. They write, *"We communicate our interpersonal expectancies and biases through very subtle, almost imperceptible, non-verbal cues. These cues are so subtle that they are neither encoded nor decoded at an intentional, conscious level of awareness [...] Thin Slices of behavior provide a great deal of information and permit significantly accurate predictions."*[72] Not only are we judged on the first impression we make, these impressions are rather accurate.

We are intuitive animals. We have the ability to know things without reasoning. Part of our brain operates quickly and subconsciously, providing instant responses based on what we learned in the past. Malcolm Gladwell describes intuition as "rapid cognition."[73] The idea for writing *Blink: The Power of Thinking Without Thinking* came to Gladwell after he grew out his hair and realized that it triggered absurd stereotypes about him. One of the book's conclusions is that the ability to quickly filter cues is common to great decision makers.

In a study carried out by Nicolas O. Rule and Nalini Ambadi, pictures of CEOs from the 25 highest and 25 lowest ranked companies were extracted from their 2006 listing on the Fortune 500 website. Undergraduates were asked to assess the leadership, power, trustworthiness, and reliability of the individuals pictured. In order to make the data uniform, the chosen CEOs were all male, in same age group, equally attractive, and all unknown to

---

[72] Nalini Ambady and Robert Rosenthal, "Thin Slices of Expressive Behavior as Predictors of Interpersonal Consequences: A Meta-Analysis," *Psychological Bulletin* 111, No. 2 (1992), 256-274.

[73] Malcolm Gladwell, *Blink: The Power of Thinking Without Thinking* (New York: Little, Brown and Company, 2005).

the undergraduates. According to Rule and Ambadi, " ... *naïve judgments provided more accurate assessments of individuals than well-informed judgments can.*" For instance, undergraduates were able to determine the financial success of CEOs through facial appearance.[74]

Humans aren't the only ones capable of making these snap judgments. A computer can predict the outcome of a negotiation after 5 minutes of analyzing conversational dynamics of parties attending a meeting.[75] I think that there will soon be a time when robots will be assisting negotiators in reading others, combining analysis of body language, physiology, eye movement, etc.[76] Apple, Google, Facebook, and others spend billions of dollars to build robots who can read us better.[77]

⌈IN ESSENCE⌋

- Negotiation starts before you enter a meeting room.
- The more you have in common with someone, the more likely that person will be to find you sympathetic and relatable.
- Do your homework on the people and entities you are dealing with before negotiating and turn it to your advantage. Don't leave negotiation meetings to fate.
- The most valuable and lasting negotiators aren't primarily driven by bonuses or other flashy incentives. They first see themselves as problem solvers and create value for themselves and others.

---

[74] Nicholas O. Rule and Nalini Ambady, "The Face of Success: Inferences from Chief Executive Officers' Appearance Predict Company Profits," *Psychological Science*, Volume 19 – Number 2, February 1, 2008, 109-111.

[75] Jared R. Curhan and Alex Pentland, "Thin Slices of Negotiation: Predicting Outcomes from Conversational Dynamics Within the First 5 Minutes," *Journal of Applied Psychology*, 2007, Vol. 92, No. 3, 802– 811.

[76] Sabrina Hoppe, Tobias Loetscher, Stephanie A. Morey, and Andreas Bulling, "Eye Movements During Everyday Behavior Predict Personality Traits," *Frontiers in Human Neuroscience*, April 13, 2018.

[77] Lisa Barrett, "Smile if you think robots can read our emotions," *The Financial Times*, April 5, 2017.

- Your attitude and physiology are key to succeed in negotiation. Align your body and mind into a state of positivity before negotiation starts.
- Be focused. Make a conscious decision and limit the excessive load of information and distractions surrounding you.
- Practicing meditation as little as 10 minutes a day helps to reduce stress level, increase focus and energy, and heighten level of awareness.
- If you can't see the chinks in your armor, they may cost you dearly.
- Practice self-awareness and take time to think without ruminating. Ask the question "what?" instead of "why?"
- Get feedback from others, but do this tactfully.
- Confidence should not be confused with arrogance or stubbornness.
- We are judged on the first impression we make, and they tend to be accurate. Always make a good first impression while remaining authentic.

CHAPTER THREE:

Evolving in the Modern World

Places don't matter to people anymore. Places aren't the point. People are only ever half present where they are these days. They always have at least one foot in the great digital nowhere.

—Matt Haig[78]

Evolving in a modern world offers a myriad of opportunities to negotiators but also great challenges. In the last few decades, a great number of new technologies have emerged, offering us easier solutions, while creating a paradox in which those solutions simplify our lives even as they complicate our lives. The comfort of facile communications should not make us forget the most basic principles of human nature, the understanding of which is key to succeed at negotiation.

Our reach is now global, and the world is borderless. This new world is complex and requires negotiators to develop proper abilities and mindset. It also carries an evil: stress. We face an overload of information and tasks in a context of constant deadlines. Stress mitigation strategies are crucial for negotiators who want to succeed at influencing others.

---

[78] Matt Haig, *How to Stop Time: A Novel* (Great Britain, Canongate Books Ltd, 2017)

[12] The Evil of Our Time

> How much pain have cost us the evils which have never happened?
> —Thomas Jefferson[79]

Our world is a stressful place for many of us. Some say stress is a response to adversity – it compels us to focus, to be responsive in the face of challenge. It certainly can do this, but excessive stress is not good for a negotiator. The constant pressure of demanding time constraints may elicit an overstress that can impair a negotiator's performance, patience, and judgment.

Stress makes it more difficult to control our emotions and clouds our ability to sense the emotions of others. Some emotions like fear and anger can cause or elevate it, creating a vicious circle. In this context, emotional intelligence is crucial[80] to avoid difficulties and counter a wise opponent who would play our weakness to their own advantage.

Long working hours are a common cause of stress. A negotiator, especially an international one, often works many hours. Employers frequently assess dedication based on the time their employees spend on the job, their availability, and other factors that encourage shunning the 9-to-5 mentality in favor of a more demanding schedule. If you're an entrepreneur, the line between your professional and personal life is likely very thin. Constant work can create a downward spiral starting with eating poorly, drinking more alcohol, or engaging in other unhealthy habits to cope with an exhausting schedule.

Business or political leaders also work long hours. *"Could I work 130 hours in a week?"* Marissa Mayer, ex-CEO of Yahoo!, asked herself in a *Bloomberg*

---

[79] Thomas Jefferson Randolph, *Correspondence and Miscellanies from the Papers of Thomas Jefferson*, Volumes 3 and 4 (Charlottesville, F. Carr, And Co., 1829), 271.

[80] Candace M. Raio et al. "Cognitive emotion regulation fails the stress test," *Proceedings of the National Academy of Sciences of the United States of America* 110(37) 2013: 15139-44.

Businessweek interview. *"The answer is yes, if you're strategic about when you sleep, when you shower, and how often you go to the bathroom."*[81] According to an interview given to Bill O'Reilly in 2017, Donald Trump only sleeps 4 to 5 hours a night.[82] French President Emmanuel Macron is also known to sleep very little.[83]

Despite the glorification of excessive work, the reality is that constant work and sleep deprivation aren't healthy. These deficiencies cause performance to suffer in the long run. Such a lifestyle contributes to stress, which in turn has been proven to exacerbate diseases such as depression, high blood pressure, heart attacks, etc.[84,85]

When one is involved in complex negotiations, long hours may be impossible to avoid. However, even in the most demanding cases, greater efficiency can be found through balance. Quality sleep, power naps, meditation, and a healthy diet are worth the time investment.

The barrage of data to which we're constantly subjected is also a major cause of stress. Overwhelmed by too much information to process, our brains get overstimulated and are unable to cope. We end up in a situation of chronic unresolved problems and, ultimately, anxiety.

Don't get me wrong – it's important to stay connected in this new world. But being too connected can cause mental fatigue. Find time to pause and leave your smartphone behind. Disconnecting during meals is a great place to start.

---

[81] "Yahoo's Marissa Mayer on Selling a Company While Trying to Turn It Around," Interview with Max Chafkin, *Bloomberg Businessweek,* August 4, 2016.

[82] Dennis Michael Lynch, "Trump Only Gets a Few Hours of Sleep Each Night," YouTube Video, Posted on February 8, 2017. https://www.youtube.com/watch?v=kZkm-CHA67o&feature=youtu.be.

[83] "'Je dors peu,' confie Emmanuel Macron à Laurent Delahousse," Video, Published December 17, 2017, https://www.francetvinfo.fr/politique/emmanuel-macron/video-je-dors-peu-confie-emmanuel-macron-a-laurent-delahousse_2519219.html

[84] Kyungjin Lee et al. "The impact of long working hours on psychosocial stress response among white-collar workers," *Industrial Health,* vol. 55,1 (2016): 46-53.

[85] Sheldon Cohen, Denise Janicki-Deverts, William J. Doyle, Gregory E. Miller, Ellen Frank, Bruce S. Rabin, and Ronald B. Turner, "Chronic stress, glucocorticoid receptor resistance, inflammation, and disease risk," PNAS, April 17, 2012, 109 (16), 5995-5999.

Another major contributor to stress is the constant scramble for money, status, and recognition, or what some call the rat race. The desire for growth and profit are two of the major cogs in the machine of the modern world. In such a climate, it's no wonder that we feel the need to work toward these goals, set high expectations, and worry about how to spend our time most profitably.

Working more can make us rich and increase our social standing, but these gains can come at the cost of us having less time for ourselves and losing balance in our personal lives. Many of us keep ourselves engrossed in work and busy developing multitasking skills in order to acquire more goods and services, but we can't get more than 24 hours a day. Quality time for yourself is a priceless commodity and worth seeking. Less stress makes you more focused on what really matters and, therefore, more efficient.

Deadlines are another common cause of stress in the business world. We're urged by deadlines to respond instantaneously. Savvy marketers have learned to create ads that mimic this sense of urgency ("Buy now! Early bird!"). In the workplace, we are told that deadlines help us cope with a heavy workload and prioritize our time. However, we all receive emails and messages tagged "urgent" or "important," not so much because they are, but because their senders are worried that we won't read or respond to them otherwise. Emails are a primary cause of stress at work. If you're able to resist an unnecessary and immediate response while engaging in longer sessions of unbroken activity, you'll perform better, be more productive, and probably be less stressed.

Deadlines are necessary to get things moving, and a strict timeline, if properly applied, can make all parties more responsive. The same applies to ultimatums, which can also be an effective negotiating tactic (preferably used as a last resort considering the threat they carry). In 1908, psychologists Robert Yerkes and John Dillingham Dodson demonstrated that performance increases with psychological or mental arousal.[86] But these pressures should

---

[86] Robert M. Yerkes and John D. Dodson, "The Relation of Strength of Stimulus to Rapidity of Habit-formation," *Journal of Comparative Neurology and Psychology*, 18 (1908): 459-482.

only be exercised when truly necessary – harsh deadlines should not become standard procedure. While a quick response is often required, negotiators shouldn't forget that patience is also a virtue. We have developed a culture of impatience and instant gratification. The Internet has connected us to a degree unprecedented in human history. It's given us access to a quality and breadth of information that, only a few decades ago, would have taken us ages to find and analyze. We take this extraordinary moment for granted sometimes and get frustrated when we have to wait more than a few seconds for a video to load.

In this context, it is not surprising to hear science tell us that negotiators end up relying more and more on stereotypes, common sense, and intuitive judgments to close deals.[87] Stress propelled by too much information, a multiplication of deadlines, and the feeling that we are always short of time make us take hastier, if not regretful, decisions.

[13] Technology Changes Us

> Once a new technology rolls over you, if you're not part of the steamroller, you're part of the road.
>
> —Stewart Brand[88]

Technology has changed the way we think, behave, and interact. It's helped us to overcome time and efficiency difficulties and improved our lives in many ways. New tools have exposed us to new cultures and greater networks.

Because we're caught in the middle of important transformations, many of us aren't able to see the vast societal and cultural changes affected by these new developments. We saw earlier that the Internet can generate stress, distraction,

---

[87] Carsten K. W. De Dreu, "Time pressure and closing of the mind in negotiation," *Organizational Behavior and Human Decision Processes,* 91 (2003): 280–295.

[88] Stewart Brand, *The Media Lab: Inventing the Future at MIT* (New York: Viking Penguin Inc, 1987), 9.

and even isolation. Another example is how social media influences the way we make decisions. We seek information, discussion, and opinions on these platforms to validate our decisions, and sometimes our biases.

Smartphones and computers are technologies that have become essential and ubiquitous in nearly every area of life, including negotiation. When starting a new job, these tools are some of the first any executive receives. Today, e-negotiation is not only acceptable but viewed as a standard (whether via email, social media, or text messaging). There are many benefits to e-negotiation. We don't have to be in the same room. It is possible to communicate instantly with someone on the other side of the globe. Questions can be asked and answers obtained at the speed of light. Thanks to cloud computing, we can make accessible and exchange volumes of data at the tap of a button.

Although e-negotiation provides greater convenience, it also presents its own challenges. Because of the increase in speed, you'd think that e-negotiations would shorten the bargaining process, but this isn't always the case. Misunderstandings occur more often over email than in person, and the possibility of distraction and loss of focus is often greater when you're communicating online. Face-to-face negotiation creates more rapport and cooperation. Rapport encourages better outcomes. This does not mean that electronic communication is bad for negotiating. In fact, it's a necessity in the actual world, but there are limitations and dangers that a negotiator should consider. Overreliance on online communication may create more problems than it solves.

Context is much more difficult to determine in writing than face-to-face. Lack of context can easily land correspondents in hot water if they're not careful. For instance, the person you are writing an email to may be experiencing a bad day. An abrupt email may just add to their stress. Email lacks cues, like facial expression and vocal tone, that allow us to read the other party. Perceiving negative emotions with some degree of accuracy is an important factor in negotiation. It allows us to adjust our approach to others and the right timing for it.

In one of their research studies, psychologists Jennifer Parlamis and Daniel Ames found that *"email dyads have less pro-social concerns, are less likely to reach an agreement, less satisfied with the quality of the interaction during the negotiation, reported less rapport and rated future trust in their partner significantly lower than face-to-face dyads."*[89] You may have also noticed that cooperation between two people involved in electronic communications increases when they share photos, personal information, or already know each other.

Instant communication generates a sense of urgency and encourages us to be less careful with what we write. Many, when communicating online, forget some of the most basic principles of human interaction. I'm not talking about typos, grammatical errors, or the trail of emails we sometimes forget to remove before pressing the "send" button. Before you post or send that important email or text, take time to review it and allow your emotions to be filtered. You should always remain polite and make sure that your responses aren't triggered by emotions, such as contempt or anger. Allow yourself the chance to read over what you've written, out loud if possible. Professional emails or messages should carry more information than emotion. They should be brief and clear. For very sensitive, long, complicated, or emotionally charged matters, it is preferable to meet in person or have a conversation via the phone. Once the essential details have been ironed out, you can send a confirmation email.

Also bear in mind that messages and emails can mean more than what they literally say. We often overestimate our capacity to read and decode them. It's important to develop an ability to read between the lines. People often hide behind the language they use in writing. Many are actually more inclined to use tougher tactics (or even lie) when not negotiating face-to-face.

---

[89] Jennifer Parlamis and Daniel Ames, "Face-to-Face and Email Negotiations: A Comparison of Emotions, Perceptions and Outcomes," Paper Presented at the 23rd Annual International Association of Conflict Management Conference, Boston, Massachusetts, June 24-27, 2010.

Electronic communications can be useful to keep a paper trail, but they can also be used against those who give their word carelessly. In an interview with Patrick Bet-David, American entrepreneur Mark Cuban, an avid user of emails, discussed how his emails were taken out of context and used as evidence against him when the SEC accused him of insider trading.[90] In one of the emails, he recommended that a friend not invest in a specific stock. Cuban claimed that his remarks were mischaracterized. He spent considerable time and effort clearing his name.

In some areas of the world, employers or the government can gain access to your emails and messages. The European Court of Human Rights, for example, ruled that employers can have access to workers' private emails.[91]

With every major shift in technology, the rules of the game can change for negotiators. Some technology becomes so ubiquitous that resisting it is not an option. Rather than ignoring new technologies, negotiators should perpetually broaden their knowledge and their skill sets to stay ahead of the curve, but with discernment. A negotiator cannot afford being left behind. Most people keep the software on their devices updated, but few take time to work on themselves with the same consistency.

By reducing the risk of fraud and simplifying money transfer (just to mention a couple of benefits), cryptocurrency has revolutionized the way money is used. Although banks currently treat cryptocurrency as a mere commodity, cryptocurrency and blockchain should be of great interest to any negotiator because of their growing importance in transactions.

Artificial intelligence will be the next "big" thing as well, with robots replacing humans in many aspects of our lives including increasingly complex tasks. Artificial intelligence is a group of algorithms able to modify themselves or create new ones. This ability to grow by itself is called intelligence. Computers will soon be creative enough to draft contracts, research, negotiate for us,

---

[90] "Mark Cuban: Best Interview UNCENSORED," YouTube Video, 57:42, "Valuetainment." November 23, 2015, https://www.youtube.com/watch?v=S8yjzUqK1zQ/.

[91] Laura Hughes, "Bosses can snoop on workers' private emails and messages, European court rules," *The Telegraph,* January 13, 2016.

and assist in reaching win-win outcomes (provided they are not programmed to be deceptive).[92] It will likely be the case in the fields of hiring or bidding, for instance. Emotion-recognition technologies and profiling algorithms have already been developed as a tool for recruiters to assess candidates.

Movies try to scare us with stories of robots taking over, but reality is still far from this fiction. The human brain is extremely complex, and it has not been fully decoded yet. I share the views of some psychologists. The human brain is characterized by the functions of understanding and willingness. Robots don't develop willingness. They follow a set of rules and do what we ask them to do. AI will probably never completely replace human interactions, but it will become an effective assistant tool. Negotiators must be prepared.

No matter how many new opportunities technology creates for us, basic principles of human communication should never be forgotten. Along his prodigious career, Winston Churchill had an agenda full of meetings, conferences (both at home and abroad), teas, dinners, and even picnics (some during the time of war). Although telegrams and radio conversations could have been an easy and convenient form of communication for him, he sought personal contact all his busy life and employed his knowledge, eloquence, and considerable charm to influence his ever-widening circle. We can take a lesson from him.

---

[92] Tim Baarslag, Michael Kaiser, Enrico H. Gerding, Catholijn M. Jonker, and Jonathan Gratch, "When Will Negotiation Agents Be Able to Represent Us? The Challenges and Opportunities for Autonomous Negotiators," Paper presented at Proceedings of the Twenty-Sixth International Joint Conference on Artificial Intelligence, Melbourne, August 19, 2017.

[14] The World Is a Global Village

> There are not more than five primary colors, yet in combination they produce more hues than can ever been seen.
> There are not more than five cardinal tastes, yet combinations of them yield more flavors than can ever be tasted.
>
> —Sun Tzu[93]

As the *Boston Globe* and *Financial Times* respectively put it, *the world is now a global village fostered by cheap, speedy and convenient communication and to argue against the global economy is like stating opposition to the weather – it continues whether you like it or not.*[94,95]

After a century tainted with major conflicts, nationalism, protectionism, and the fall of the Berlin Wall in 1989, a free flow of goods, services, capital, technologies, and people has been encouraged in search for social harmony and progress. New technologies, starting with the Internet, have offered great opportunities with people, new markets, and information now a click away from us. Social media has exposed us, with an unprecedented level, to other cultures, communities, and new friends.

Tariffs and barriers have been lowered in many countries to welcome investors, workforce, and talents from overseas. Many multinationals, which employ a great part of the world's population today, optimize their businesses by transferring production, staff, offices, or headquarters to other countries (sometimes after being incentivized to do so).

---

[93] Sun Tzu, *The Art of War,* originally published in 1910. (New York: Cosimo, Inc., 2010), 14.

[94] Nicholas Carr, "How Tech Created a Global Village — and Put Us at Each Other's Throats," *The Boston Globe,* April 21, 2017.

[95] Senator John McCain, "Donald Trump Retreats from Trade Deals at His Peril," *The Financial Times,* December 6, 2016.

Competition has been fostered to offer people a variety of international products and services which can, in a few days, if not instantaneously, be shipped to you. Transport is now more accessible with global air traffic increasing every year to possibly reach the astonishing number of 8.2 billion travelers in 2037, according to the International Air Transport Association. Negotiators can afford to fly many miles for a couple of hours of meetings and be back home the same day to kiss their children good night, unless they decide to negotiate online with someone they will never meet.

Western economies are so interconnected now that untying the knots cannot happen without substantial risks and challenges. When a multinational such as HSBC is sentenced in 2012 to pay a $1.9 billion US fine for money laundering and faces criminal charges in the US, it quickly becomes a major political issue and a threat for the entire world's economy due to the size of HSBC's global spiderweb.[96] The 2008 financial crisis and Brexit are other perfect examples of how economies have become integrated over time.

As with everything, there are pros and cons when it comes to globalization. However, its effects and challenges for a negotiator are not arguable. Regardless of the high level of assimilation associated with globalization bolstered by technology, negotiators must understand that the world continues to embrace a diversity of ethnicities, social-cultural groups, nations, and civilizations. Some people continue to share a common way of life and interact differently with other cultures. They share and cherish a language, practices, customs, and a common history. They adopt meaning systems, codes, beliefs, and ideas they follow or conform to. Geert Hofstede, Dutch social psychologist, rightly described culture as the "software of the mind."[97] Without a cultural mapping, it would actually be difficult for all of us to process and cope with the flow of information we face daily.[98] Therefore, these cultural references are necessary.

---

[96] Glenn Greenwald, "HSBC, Too Big to Jail, Is the New Poster Child for US Two-tiered Justice System," *The Guardian*, December 12, 2012.

[97] Geert Hofstede, Gert Jan Hofstede, and Michael Minkov, *Cultures and Organizations: Software of the Mind* (New York: MCGraw-Hill, 2010).

[98] Edward T. Hall, *Beyond Culture* (New York: Anchor Books, 1976).

No matter the force of globalization, and although cultures may be affected on the surface, they continue to flow in people's veins with variable intensity. Very few people are truly unrooted in the business world. Ignoring or forgetting about cultural identities when negotiating would be a mistake.

Because we all end up consuming the same products, watching the same movies, listening to the same music, or even speaking English, some may think that it will soon be the end of diversity and the rise of one global culture. The same people may feel that cultural differences have been ironed out. Although there is no doubt that cultures are influenced by external factors and evolve over time, forming cultural groups is in human nature. People still aggregate, hardwired to a core of commonality.

Everyday life provides examples of cultural failures in this world. Mergers between foreign entities are one of the most eloquent examples. A famous disaster was the merger between Daimler and Chrysler in late 1990s. At the time, both companies called it a "merger of equals." In reality, it was a cultural clash between Germans and Americans at all levels. Both companies tried to get along for 10 years, but ultimately split in 2007, when Daimler sold Chrysler to Cerberus Capital Management.[99] *"We obviously overestimated the potential of synergies ... I don't know if any amount of due diligence could have given us a better estimation in that regard,"* Dieter Zetsche, chief executive of Daimler Chrysler, said at a news conference.[100] The merger encountered significant cultural differences from the start. *"You had two companies from different countries with different languages and different styles coming together yet there were no synergies. It was simply an exercise in empire-building,"* said Dave Healy, analyst with Burnham Securities.

Work assignment abroad can be another example of cultural clash with expatriates returning to their country of origin earlier than anticipated for poor performance or maladaptation. Many factors can explain such failures, from cultural shock to mismatched staffing, family issues, or the false

---

[99] Danny Hakim, "You Say 'Takeover.' I Say 'Merger of Equals.'" *The New York Times,* December 21, 2003.

[100] Jim Mateja, "How Chrysler Marriage Failed," *Chicago Tribune,* May 15, 2007.

assumption from the employer that an individual performing at home will perform abroad. Expatriates carrying frustration, anger, and anguish overseas are usually those who will have the most difficulties adjusting to other cultures.

A category of negotiators will, under the pressure of harsh deadlines and full agendas, rush to get their flights, reach their destinations, and get themselves locked in a meeting for a couple of hours, tired and with a mere sandwich as carburant in their stomach. They miss the opportunity of building solid bridges between their own culture and the one they are visiting. They mistake the cultural gap and incompatibility of character as the reasons for their poor performance instead of looking inward at the social pressures that are distracting them or preventing them from having the right approach.

Erin Meyer, author of *The Culture Map*, shares this opinion when she writes that *"millions of people work in global settings while reviewing everything from their own cultural perspectives and assuming that all differences, controversy, and misunderstanding are rooted in personality. This is not due to laziness. Many well-intentioned people don't educate themselves about cultural differences because they believe that if they focus on individual differences, that will be enough."*[101]

Cultures impact a negotiation's outcomes. They influence the behaviors of negotiators adopting them. Everybody comes to meetings with their own cultural luggage, some having bigger baggage than others.

When you face a culture that is not your own, you add another layer of complexity to social interactions. Poorly planned cross-border negotiations can consume significant time, lead to painful mistakes, and be costly. To succeed as a negotiator in a global world, a global mindset is required.

---

[101] Erin Meyer, *The Culture Map* (New York: Public Affairs, 2014), 12.

[15] Global Mindset Required

> You must be shapeless, formless, like water. When you pour water in a cup, it becomes the cup. When you pour water in a bottle, it becomes the bottle. When you pour water in a teapot, it becomes the teapot. Water can drip and it can crash. Become like water, my friend.
>
> —Bruce Lee[102]

The *Financial Times* gave an excellent definition of a global mindset in its online Lexicon: *"one that combines an openness to and awareness of diversity across cultures and markets with a propensity and ability to see common patterns across countries and markets."*

Developing a global mindset requires certain assets within the reach of anyone prepared to put in a bit of effort. The first asset is an *open mind*, which includes curiosity and the acknowledgment of and willingness to engage with other cultures. The second asset is *knowledge* and what we learn about other cultures, including differences, traditions, history, and more. The third asset is a *valuable international network* and a capacity to activate it efficiently. Missing just one of these elements could cause a negotiator to be less impactful in cross-border negotiations.

The mindset consists of building cultural bridges, understanding subtle differences from one market or culture to another, and quickly identifying valid trade-offs and opportunities.

The ability to gain trust from foreigners is key in this context. The reality is that we all tend to trust people from our own culture more than those from another and are impaired by our own cultural biases. This is a challenge, and it requires us to take a step back. We often prejudge other populations compared to or based on our culture or values, and this prejudgment affects

---

[102] Bruce Lee and John Little. *Bruce Lee: A Warrior's Journey.* Documentary Film. Directed by John Little. Los Angeles: Warner Home Video, 2000.

economic exchange. Perceptions rooted in culture can be misleading, especially when two cultures have a history of conflicts or have few similarities.[103] Out of bias some people believe, for instance, that Chinese businesses are worse creditors than Australian or British ones. Research confirms this bias is false.[104] Consequences can be important: a negotiator may be overly careful, requesting additional guarantees from a Chinese counterpart, slowing the negotiation process down. A corporation may prefer to work with Australian businesses rather than a Chinese one for an equivalent service or product to their own detriment because of this unfounded cultural bias.

One way to measure a global mindset is by the quality of an international network. How many valuable relationships have you been able to develop abroad, not just exchanging business cards and friending people on social media? How many of these contacts come to you naturally for opportunities or advice without you chasing them? The greater the number, the better chance your mindset is global.

The ideal scenario to develop a global mindset is to be exposed at an early age to other cultures, study abroad, and learn multiple languages. Sadly, not everyone has this opportunity. The education we receive and the country we originate from play a significant role in how much effort we must invest to foster a global mindset. Coming from a large country like the US, which lies between two massive oceans, can limit your chances of exposure to a diversity of cultures. Fewer than half of the US population actually has a valid passport. Compare that with being born in tiny Luxembourg, considered one of the most multilingual countries on the planet.

Some of us can have a head start, but acquiring a global mindset is more a question of attitude than aptitude. Whether at an early age or later on in our lives, learning or becoming familiar with foreign languages should be an esteemed goal. A foreign language is the door to another culture. "The limits of my language mean the limits of my world," said Ludwig Wittgenstein,

---

[103] Luigi Guiso, Paola Sapienza, and Luigi Zingales, "Cultural Bias in Economic Exchange," Centre for Economic Policy Research, London, January 2005.

[104] MarketInvoice, "The State of Late Payment", 2016.

Austrian-born philosopher.[105]

We certainly cannot learn all the languages in this world, although some of us are impressive and have a few under our belts. Regardless, efforts can be made to learn and understand some basics, and with technologies including language apps, acquisition is more attainable than ever before.

Negotiators engaging with other cultures should no longer ignore the ramifications of languages. This truth goes far beyond the mere translation of words. Through a foreign language, it is not only possible to understand the way foreigners think, but also incorporate, in some ways, their thinking. Benjamin Lee Whorf, famous American linguist, thought that *"language can influence thoughts and that it is not merely a reproducing instrument for voicing ideas but rather the shaper of ideas, the program and guide for the individual's mental activity."*[106]

For instance, some scientists have proven a link between the structure of language and the propensity for a population speaking that language to save money. Keith Chen, professor of economics, UCLA Anderson School of Management, explains in his Ted Talk that a language, by the nature of its structure, can force you to think and provide information you wouldn't do in another language. He also explains that speakers using a language with no future tense (such as Estonians or Finns) are 30 percent more likely to save in any year and retire with 25 percent more savings. They procrastinate less.[107]

Although there is never a bad time to start learning or becoming familiar with additional languages, one should be aware that the capacity to learn them declines with age. This decline is not only because the younger generations absorb knowledge like a sponge and older generations process more slowly. Kids often just have more time, deal with fewer daily responsibilities,

---

[105] Ludwig Wittgenstein, *Tractatus Logico-Philosophicus* (New York: Cosimo Classics, 2007), 5.6.

[106] Benjamin Lee Whorf, *Science and Linguistics* (Cambridge, Massachusetts: Technology Review, 1940), 42:229-231, 247-248, no. 6.

[107] Keith Chen, "Could Language Affect Your Ability to Save Money?" TEDGlobal, June 2012, 11:58, https://www.ted.com/talks/keith_chen_could_your_language_affect_your_ability_to_save_money/.

and often have greater motivation than adults.[108]

Language is not limited to verbal language. Body language can also be culturally specific. The Japanese bow is a good example. Many people have heard of it, but not many know that the level of inclination of the body has different meanings. Length of hold is also an important mark of respect. Although we can sometimes be forgiven for our ignorance, the use of inappropriate body language can have adverse consequences either back home when interacting with foreigners or when visiting other cultures.[109] A thumbs-up in Iran has the same significance as an extended middle finger in the US, just for your information.

Time, feedback, disagreements, respect, and so on are often expressed differently from one culture to another. German and Scandinavian individuals tend to send straightforward messages. Asian individuals send some with more room for interpretation. Things are left unsaid because their culture is supposed to explain the rest. The information is less in the written message than in the context of the culture or the person who sent it.

There is a myriad of cultures in this world with all kinds of particularities, but many will share common features. Traditionally, cultures are divided into monochronic ones or polychronic ones. For monochronic cultures time is regarded as linear, and people do one thing at a time. In monochronic cultures lateness and interruptions are not well tolerated. Polychronic cultures perceive time as more flexible. Punctuality is less important, and interruptions are acceptable.

Germany, Switzerland, Scandinavia, Netherlands, and Japan have monochronic cultures. Punctual completion of the job or a repayment of a loan can be vital elements of a contract. The Japanese take it to another level, where you should not only be on time but be there earlier as a mark of respect.

---

[108] Nienke Meulman, Martijn Wieling, Simone A. Sprenger, Laurie A. Stowe, and Monika S. Schmid, (2015), "Age Effects in L2 Grammar Processing as Revealed by ERPs and How (Not) to Study Them." PLoS ONE 10(12): e0143328.

[109] Associated Press, "Obama's Bow in Japan Sparks Some Criticism." NBCnews.com, November 16, 2009.

Polychronic countries are found in Southern Europe, the Middle East, and South America. People there will look at doing as much they can in one day and will feel efficient if they do so. Therefore, coming late to a meeting is not such a big issue. Relationships are valued over time in the Middle East. Mismatches appear when negotiators pay more attention to their watch than to people they deal with.

In many Asian and African nations, the concept of time is neither monochronic nor polychronic; it is cyclical. In Africa the natural cycle of time (e.g., crops and agriculture) controls people, rather than people controlling time. The sun rises every day, and there is plenty of time in China. This does not mean that the Chinese don't value time; being late to a meeting can still be rude in China. Rather, Chinese value patience over punctuality. They walk around a pool to make the right decision. Patience is a key component of Chinese culture, and prolongation rather than immediacy is paramount.

Proverbs can tell a lot about a cultural mindset. Here are some charming and telling examples:

Stay a while, lose a mile. (Dutch proverb)
A stitch in time saves nine. (UK proverb)
What flares up fast will extinguish sooner. (Turkish proverb)
Time is the master of those who have no other master. (Arabian proverb)
With time and patience, the mulberry leaf becomes a silk gown. (Chinese proverb)

In his book *When Cultures Collide*,[110] Richard D. Lewis classifies cultures in 3 significant categories:

- **Linear-Active Attributes** (e.g., German, Swiss, Swedes). They are introverted, patient, punctual, less emotional, follow procedures, rarely interrupt, and stick to the plan, etc.

---

[110] Richard D. Lewis, *When Cultures Collide: Leading Across Cultures* (Boston: Nicholas Brealey Publishing, 2006).

- **Multi-Active Attributes** (e.g., Italian, Spanish, Hispanic Americans). They are extroverted, impatient, talkative, work any hours, not punctual, change plans, emotional, inquisitive, etc.
- **Reactive Attributes** (e.g., Japanese, Chinese, Vietnamese). They are introverted, patient, silent, respectful, punctual, good listeners, see whole picture, protect face, plan slowly, avoid confrontation, etc.

When including Arabs and Africans as part of the Multi-Active people, the Multi-Active group represents a majority of people on earth. Other cultures navigate around these 3 poles. The French will be between Linear-Active and Multi-Active but closer to Multi-Active. Canadians will be between Linear-Active and Reactive. Indians will be between Multi-Active and Reactive.

This section is not intended to identify every difference between cultures but to provide you with fundamental principles and some guidance in how you shape your global mindset. Your job as a negotiator is to become culturally intelligent by being aware, curious, and knowledgeable about cultural subtleties. You should, at a minimum, know about the geopolitical, economic, and financial games being played on the surface of this planet and their impact and ramifications in countries other than your own. The broader your cultural spectrum is, the better you will be at decoding international affairs and connecting the dots in this complex world.

Negotiators who stay in the comfort zone of their own cultures, without acknowledging cultural nuances of others, see the world mostly through their own cultural lens. To remain ethnocentric is to surrender to the lesser aspects of human nature. Assuming the world is turning global anyway is a flawed approach that limits opportunities, growth, and success. While balancing and preserving their inner harmony, negotiators should adapt and soften their edges to fit into a world of incredible diversity. *Become like water, my friend.*

⌈IN ESSENCE⌋

- Stress compels us to focus but can also impair performance, patience, and judgment. If you come to the bargaining table overstressed, you compromise your emotional intelligence.
- Constant work and sleep deprivation are unhealthy and cause performance to suffer in the long run. Quality sleep, power naps, meditation, and a healthy lifestyle are worth the time investment.
- Being too connected electronically causes mental fatigue. Find time to pause and reflect.
- Overcommunication by email and instant messages can create more problems than it solves.
- Technology should be your servant, not your master.
- Don't overestimate your capacity to read and decode emails and messages. Remember written communication is often missing important context and cues.
- Negotiation has a better chance at success and efficiency if it happens face-to-face.
- Make sure that your written responses aren't triggered by emotions. Professional emails should carry more information than emotion.
- We have developed a culture of impatience and instant gratification. Harsh deadlines should not become standard negotiation protocol.
- Regardless of new opportunities technology creates for us, never underestimate the basic principles of human communication.
- Perpetually broaden your base of knowledge – and your skill set, technological and otherwise – to stay ahead of the curve.
- No matter the force of globalization, cultures will continue flowing in people's veins with variable intensity. Very few people are truly unrooted in the business world.
- To succeed in a global world, a global mindset is required.

- Developing a global mindset requires an open mind, knowledge, and a valuable international network.
- Many negotiators wrongly think that the cultural gap and incompatibility of character are the reasons for their poor performance in an international world.
- Language is not merely a reproducing instrument for voicing ideas but rather the shaper of ideas.
- The broader your cultural spectrum is, the better you will be decoding international affairs and connecting the dots.
- *Become like water, my friend.*

CHAPTER FOUR:
About Human Nature

Human action can be modified to some extent, but human nature cannot be changed.

—Abraham Lincoln[111]

Being a successful negotiator presupposes a great understanding of human nature. Influence is key in negotiation. Changing what people believe or desire is the objective of every negotiator. However, human nature remains underlying. There are indelible ways humans think and behave, and even if some aspects of human nature are less pronounced in some of us, there are still common patterns, which should be well assimilated.

---

[111] Full text: Abraham Lincoln's Cooper Union Address of February 27, 1860, New York, *New York Times*, May 2, 2004.

⌈16⌋ Mind Body Language

My body is a stubborn child, my language is a very civilized adult.
—Roland Barthes[112]

Body language is one of the main ways that human beings use to communicate. It refers to facial expressions, postures, gestures, and mannerisms revealing our feelings, moods, or emotions. Some of these physical signals are universal (such as smiling when we are happy), while others tend to vary from culture to culture and from one individual to another.

Humans base their decisions more on what they see than on what they hear, so body language plays an important role in a negotiating process. Any in-person discussion, no matter how brief or inconsequential, involves body language. These cues may be obvious or subtle. Some cultures (like the Italian) have very expressive body language, while others (like the Finnish) are more reserved.

Many people believe that communication is largely verbal. They forget that humans, like other animals, began communicating long before the advent of language.

Albert Mehrabian, professor emeritus of psychology at UCLA, published extensively on the relative importance of verbal and nonverbal messages. He divided face-to-face communication into 3 elements:

- Words (what is actually said): 7%
- Voice (how we say the words): 38%
- Facial expressions: 55%[113]

---

[112] Roland Barthes, *A Lover's Discourse: Fragment,* (New York: Farrar, Straus and Giroux, 1978), 44.

[113] Albert Mehrabian, *Silent Messages* (Belmont, California: Wadsworth Publishing Company Inc, 1971), 43.

If you can read body language, you'll have a better chance to detect if people are lying. It's easier to lie with your words than with your body language. Discrepancies between what people are saying and how they are moving helps identify and confront liars.

The ability to read body language also gives you a better understanding of those you are dealing with and a better control of situations you experience with them. It allows you to adjust your communication strategy as the negotiation progresses.

A simple handshake, for example, can tell us a lot. It's used for greetings, salutations, and for closing deals, but it's also a sign of trust. The way you shake hands – the angle, the pressure, the length, etc. – reveals cues to others. Donald Trump's handshakes have often made headlines. Observing his technique is instructive. First, he offers a handshake by extending his hand palm up, in a submissive way – this is likely an attempt to display honesty – then, he shakes firmly and pulls the person toward him. It's an attempt to show power and dominance. The best way to respond to such a handshake is to reestablish equality by putting the right foot forward, moving toward the dominator, and daring to enter their personal space.

During negotiation, many try to hide or control their gestures and expressions (an interview for a job is a perfect example). This can be successful to some extent, but such attempts rarely fool the trained eye. Even the best actors can't hide everything. It's impossible to be conscious of all that our body is doing. Whether through an expression, a tic, or a glance, it's likely that we'll eventually give ourselves away. What is possible, though, is to be generally acquainted with physical signals and sufficiently conscious of your own cues to be able to respond appropriately and minimize the leakage of unintended messages.

If you look at pictures of John D. Rockefeller, you'll notice a calm (almost steely) demeanor. In *Titan*, a biography of Rockefeller by Ron Chernow, the subject is described as a man with *"an abnormally low pulse of fifty-two [...] Though he had honed his will into a perfect instrument, he was even-tempered by nature [...] During meetings, he was a restless doodler and note taker [...] He never lost his temper, raised a voice, uttered a profane or slang word, or acted discourteously."*[114] John D. Rockefeller was a formidable negotiator in command of his body language.

The ability to read body language provides you great indications about the thoughts, emotions, mood, and feelings of a person, but conclusions shouldn't be drawn too quickly. Body language is an indication of someone's state, but it won't always be able to tell you with certainty *why* someone is acting or feeling the way that they are. You may, for example, think that you've made someone uncomfortable, when in reality they're sick, tired, or preoccupied. For this reason, it is important to analyze a cluster of gestures and not one specifically, spot incongruences with the words spoken, and take the context into consideration.

How many negotiators can properly read the nonverbal signals others are sending? I'd venture to say that very few do, although many will say that they possess this ability. And how many of these are able to use the signals they pick up to their advantage? Even fewer.

It's not an easy task – we often get caught up in a whirlwind of stress, emotions, and distractions. We tend to forget to observe our own state and that of others: we don't pay enough attention to the signals we send and that are sent to us. We end up focusing on our thoughts and words.

Although negotiation isn't a poker game, watching poker players can be instructive for negotiators. Expert poker players usually possess great control of their body language. Their gestures and postures can be quite uniform, for instance they don't easily reveal their emotions (sometimes hiding behind sunglasses), and if they do, it is to bluff and mislead other players. The best poker players are quite observant. They can detect the emotional state of others with greater accuracy than the average person can. In his book titled *Delivering Happiness*,[115] Tony Hsieh, founder of Zappos and a poker player,

---

[114] Ron Chernow, *Titan: The Life of John D. Rockefeller, Sr.* (New York: Penguin Random House LLC, 1998), 176.

[115] Tony Hsieh, *Delivering Happiness* (New York: Business Plus, 2013), Second e-book Edition, Kindle version, Loc. 1039.

draws a parallel between business and poker. He explains how he applied to business lessons he learned from poker. One of the similarities he noticed was branding and the shaping of stories people are telling about you. He also learned that an experienced player can make 10 times as much money sitting at a table with nice mediocre players who are tired and have a lot of chips compared with sitting at a table with 9 really good players who are focused and don't have many chips in front of them. His conclusion was that in business, you should be careful with the business you choose to be in and the people you choose to deal with.

Just like expert poker players, master negotiators develop a catalogue of human signals and expressions. The human face is capable of more than 10,000 expressions according to expert Paul Ekman.[116]

The voice, the tone, the rhythm of someone's words, and the speed with which they speak are part of body language and that should never be forgotten. Unlike facial expressions, which can be faked, the voice can't be so easily simulated. It can reveal valuable information. If you know what to listen for, you'll be able to discern a speaker's emotional state. A subtle change of tone can reveal if they're stressed, angry, skeptical, or eager. When a speaker is cold angry, they'll express this anger in a less hostile manner than they would if hot angry. Their cold anger will take the form of an irritation marked by a lower acoustic pitch, increased intensity, faster attack times at voice onset, and standard rate of speech.[117]

While you're observing the way others speak, be careful to watch your own tone. There's no universal rule for what tone to use, but it's a pretty good bet that an aggressive or pushy tone won't be well received. A smile might not work every time, but, as we mentioned in Chapter 2, it's more likely to get a positive response, and may help you be more influential in talking to others.

---

[116] Paul Ekman, *Emotions Revealed* (London: Weidenfeld & Nicolson, 2003), Kindle version, Loc. 753.

[117] Federica Biassoni, Stefania Balzarotti, Micaela Giamporcaro, and Rita Ciceri, "Hot or Cold Anger? Verbal and Vocal Expression of Anger While Driving in a Simulated Anger-Provoking Scenario," SAGE Open, July-September 2016, 1-10.

Plenty of books, videos, and online courses on reading body language are available to improve a negotiator's skills. Some resources are better than others, but there's no substitute for simply taking in the other party, watching and listening instead of trying to dominate a conversation. Understand before making yourself understood.

People-watching in public places is great practice. Go to a park, a mall, a beach – anywhere that you can find a crowd of different types of people. Watch the way they interact. You may soon find that you're able to understand the substance of their conversation without hearing the words they're saying. When I'm in hotels or at restaurants by myself, I enjoy observing others discreetly. I try to guess what's going on between them by studying their body language, their appearance, and so on. This exercise also helps one to become more observant. Practice this exercise for 15 minutes a day, and you'll see marked results.

⌈17⌋ Develop Emotional Intelligence

> When dealing with people, let us remember we are not dealing with creatures of logic. We are dealing with creature of emotion, creatures bristling with prejudices and motivated by pride and vanity.
>
> —Dale Carnegie[118]

We display our emotional state with physical gestures. According to Dr. Paul Ekman, there are 7 emotions that trigger specific physical signals: anger, fear, disgust, sadness, enjoyment, surprise, and contempt.[119] Because emotions sometimes happen so quickly, they will only be visible to a carefully trained eye. Having such talent is an advantage and translates into leverage.

---

[118] Dale Carnegie, *How to Win Friends and Influence People*, Kindle, Loc. 324.

[119] Paul Ekman, *Emotions Revealed* (London: Weidenfeld & Nicolson, 2003), Kindle, Loc. 1152.

Negotiators should have some level of control over their emotions, so they don't impair their judgment or send the wrong signals to others. Yet it's hard to keep cool when there's a multimillion-dollar contract, or the fate of your company, or both, on the line. The higher the stakes, the likelier it is that we'll lose control of our emotions. Every time we heat up, we run the risk of disclosing precious information and making emotional decisions.

That doesn't mean, of course, that negotiators should be cold and clinical. Stonewalling has never been an efficient negotiation strategy. Such a tactic can trigger cautiousness in others. If they detect that you're trying to hide your emotions, you'll come across as insincere, robotic, or distant.

Sharing feelings can be beneficial sometimes. For instance, empathy has been proven to have a positive effect on negotiation. If the other party is angry, such a display of understanding can help defuse the situation.[120] Positive emotions are often contagious and have an uplifting effect on the attitudes of others. They've been proven to improve the outcome of a negotiation whereas a display of negative emotions triggers more extreme demands from counterparts.[121]

With negative emotions easily weakening your positions, it is important to refocus and remember why you're in the meeting and what your goals are. Nelson Mandela's conduct provides a great template for taking a step back. When he left prison, Mandela had every reason to be angry and resentful. He was sentenced to life and locked for many years in a tiny cell on Robben Island away from his wife, children, and friends. When he was finally free, Mandela kept his eyes on the big picture and displayed great emotional intelligence while negotiating with Frederik Willem de Klerk to bring equality to South Africa and unify the country. Without that effort, the country could

---

[120] Adam D. Galinsky, William W. Maddux, Debra Gilin, and Judith B. White. "Why It Pays to Get Inside the Head of Your Opponent: The Differential Effects of Perspective Taking and Empathy in Negotiations," *Psychological Science* 19, no. 4 (April 2008): 378–84.

[121] Shirli Kopelman, Ashleigh Shelby Rosette, and Leigh Thompson. "The three faces of Eve: Strategic displays of positive, negative, and neutral emotions in negotiations," *Organizational Behavior and Human Decision Processes* 99, Issue 1 (January 2006): 81-101.

have been torn by war.

Being emotionally intelligent in the context of negotiation means being aware of your emotions, what provokes them, to have them under minimal control, and to use them to obtain better results. You don't want your emotions making your decisions, especially in a situation where a cool head is required. Being assertive may be necessary sometimes (especially when it comes to fixing boundaries), but it should always be done with composure.

Emotions can change very quickly. We're often unaware of being overtaken until the event is occurring, or even after. It's not easy to learn to master our emotions, but there are some strategies you can use to improve your skills, starting with stress management as we tackled in Chapter 2.

Another way to train your emotional resilience is to gain an awareness of what triggers an emotional response in you. What words, attitudes, and actions from others provoke a negative reaction in you? I'm not talking about the obvious stuff – if someone's yelling at you, making you angry or on the defensive – but about subtler triggers. Perhaps, when you see the person not listening to you or checking their mobile phone while you are talking, you become overaggressive. If you take note of these changes in yourself, you'll gain a degree of self-knowledge, which can lead to emotional intelligence. If you're able to notice what's going on in yourself, you'll likely be able to see emotional shifts in other people as well.

A body sends tangible signals of emotions when they are experienced. Sweaty palms may be an indication that you're nervous or feeling stressed. If you're in a meeting and you notice that the other party has sweaty hands, it might not tell you exactly what they're thinking, but, if they're trying to come across as relaxed and collected, you'll know that the confident image they're trying to convey may not be the whole story.

Emotional reactions aren't just the result of your life experience, though your past certainly factors in to how you feel in any given situation. If you had bossy parents as a child, for example, you may be more sensitive to authority than someone raised differently. But your DNA can also influence the way you react. Research shows that we can inherit the sensitivities of our ancestors.[122]

Fear, contempt, and anger are 3 negative emotions that can derail any negotiation. These are emotions we need to keep in check when we're negotiating, and we ought to spend some time discussing each one.

FEAR

Fear breaks your focus and directs your attention to a disproportionate concern for the consequences of your actions. In such cases, you can put yourself at greater risk of making irrational decisions.

When you're afraid, your body can show it. Disturbances in your gestures and changes in your facial expressions or voice may be detected. Your weakness can become their leverage.

There are two common fears that negotiators face: fear of missing out and fear of failure.

Fear of missing out (FOMO) is defined as the fear of being left behind and missing interesting opportunities. This pushes people to make irrational decisions. FOMO can be experienced by individuals (worrying about the evolution of their career in a world of rapid changes, for instance) and organizations (worrying that their business will be disrupted or less competitive).

FOMO fills people with regret, and social networks fuel this fear by showing them things they could have done or places they could have been. It is certainly important to adapt in a world of changes and look for new trends. However, we shouldn't make changes to our way of doing things merely from fear that we will not be on top of the newest thing.

Peer input is important to decision-making. Rapidly assessing situations and opportunities is a virtue but jumping to quick conclusions is not. Problems generally arise when opportunism meets fear or impatience.

---

[122] Rebecca M. Todd, Daniel J. Müller, Daniel H. Lee, Amanda Robertson, Tayler Eaton, Natalie Freeman, Daniela J. Palombo, Brian Levine, and Adam K. Anderson. "Genes for Emotion-Enhanced Remembering Are Linked to Enhanced Perceiving," *Psychological Science* 24, no. 11 (November 2013): 2244–53.

On the other hand, *fear of failure* makes negotiators lower their goals. When this occurs, the outcome of the negotiation is generally poorer – if, that is, a commitment is made at all. Scared negotiators play it safe, as they are more concerned with losses than gains. They let fear kill their creativity. People often act rashly out of fear of embarrassment, of not being enough, of having a lot to lose, and so on.

Many executives put pressure on their employees in order to push their organizations into greater prosperity. Some will put in place strict and heavy approval processes, practice micromanagement, or even manage their business by fear. These practices can cause employees to be incapable of making decisions alone and stifle creativity at the negotiation table.

A decision made alone, especially if it isn't perceived as working out, can result in blame heaped on the decision-maker's head. It can cost a negotiator their reputation, a promotion, a bonus, a position, or even their job. A minimal degree of trust, freedom, and a reasonable margin of error (taking into consideration the experience and skills of a negotiator) should be given to those employees negotiating on behalf of organizations. Sending shy employees to negotiate without the power to make decisions is often a waste of time. In return, employees should approach negotiation well prepared, with clear objectives in mind, and a good understanding of what leverage they have and how to use it. As for entrepreneurs and business owners, they should see occasional failures as part of a learning process and as opportunities to improve (with the exception of failures due to negligence).

CONTEMPT

Contempt can be understood as a feeling of superiority toward someone to the point of rejection or exclusion. If you have contempt for someone, your body language may reveal it. You may inadvertently roll your eyes, turn away, or use language or a tone that betrays your feeling of superiority. If they spot it, it may damage (and likely destroy) whatever rapport you've built. No one likes to be looked down on, even if they made a mistake. Contempt is often mixed with anger or disgust. The perception of contempt can be limited through self-awareness practices.

Contempt is intricately linked to power. Nietzsche rightly considered that *"a passion for power is a terrible teacher that breeds great contempt."*[123] When people are negotiating with a strong power imbalance, expressions of superiority, conscious or otherwise, are common. When power is more evenly distributed, parties tend to be humbler and more respectful. Contempt arises from differences in cultural status, gender, age, descendance, etc. It can also be a reaction to a transgression of a social rule, such as a lack of respect. Cultural mistakes are quite common in international business. Be careful to not break cultural rules when you negotiate across borders. The time of colonization is over and underdeveloped countries deserve the same respect for their culture and people as other countries.

ANGER

Anger can easily be triggered during negotiation, especially when the stakes are high, the parties are tired, or when one party feels as if they're being disrespected, imposed upon, or otherwise treated unfairly. When facing aggressive behavior, it's hard for humans to not react in kind.

Anger can lead to conflict escalation and may seriously damage a relationship. This is why anger is the most dangerous of all emotions. When you speak in anger, whether you're conscious of it or not, your objective is to verbally, if not physically, harm the person you're addressing.

When you're angry, you've probably noticed that your heart beats faster, your blood pressure increases, your body temperature rises, and your face reddens. Even if you are not expressing your anger out loud, your body language can betray it. The most obvious cues are crossed arms, placing the hands on the hips to appear larger, frowning, and glaring.

Some may see strategy in anger. They falsely think that, by showing anger, it'll cause others to bend to their will, and afford them a bigger slice of the pie. However, anger during negotiation is a dangerous thing. It can cause

---

[123] Friedrich Nietzsche, *Thus Spoke Zarathustra* (New York: Dover Publications, Inc., 1999), 132.

you to let information slip that you intended to keep private, and it's almost always seen as disrespectful. You may make short-term gains through anger, but there's a good chance you'll pay for it in damage to your reputation or business. Research clearly shows that anger is counterproductive in negotiation.[124] Those who attempt to utilize anger when making deals see things in win-lose terms.

The best negotiators control their temper and direct their attention to what's most important. Dale Carnegie was wise suggesting to *"Keep calm and watch out for your first reaction. It may be you at your worst, not at your best."*[125]

Those with power or money can sometimes afford negotiating aggressively. Steve Jobs was well known for this, but such a strategy can create anger or resentment at the end.

Napoleon Bonaparte was reputed to have a very poor temper as well. He used to yell at Charles Maurice de Talleyrand-Périgord (his minister of foreign affairs at that time), who, as mentioned earlier, was well known for always reacting with composure. Napoleon insulted him many times, once going so far as to call him *"De la merde dans un bas de soie,"* which translates to *"A piece of shit in a silk stocking."*[126] Talleyrand, collected as always, told him, *"It is a shame for such a great man to be so rude."* Tactful. He may have been steaming inside, and he had every right to be, but Talleyrand's skills as a negotiator lay in controlling his emotions and directing the situation toward cooperation. Unsurprisingly, Talleyrand began supporting a change of regime when Napoleon's grip on power started to loosen.

---

[124] Keith G. Allred, John S. Mallozzi, Fusako Matsui, and Christopher P. Raia, "The Influence of Anger and Compassion on Negotiation Performance," *Organizational Behavior and Human Decision Processes,* Volume 70, Issue 3, June 1997, 175-187.

[125] Dale Carnegie, *How to Win Friends and Influence People*, Kindle, Loc. 1757.

[126] David Lawday, *Napoleon's Master: A Life of Prince Talleyrand* (London, Jonathan Cape, 2006), 2.

⌈18⌋ These Shortcuts We Take

Prejudices are what fools use for reason.

—Voltaire[127]

We humans have scripted responses, almost like computer programs, that run in the back of the brain and guide behavior automatically. We can't analyze every phenomenon we perceive, so our minds take shortcuts. We are exposed to as many as 11 million bits of information per second as we speak, but we can only process around 50 bits per second.

These shortcuts take us back to times when humans had to fight for survival and perfect their instincts. We haven't always been city-dwelling, civilized people. In a state of nature, the ability to make snap judgments, even if not completely accurate, could mean the difference between escaping a predator and becoming its lunch. The fight, flight, and freeze responses are still in us. While prejudices and biases can be different from culture to culture, many of these are rooted in the way our mind works.

Cognitive biases are systematic patterns of deviation from rationality that make us draw illogical conclusions.[128] They're basically mental errors made by oversimplifying. Most of these biases escape our conscious notice, but they can have a significant impact on our behavior. Negotiators practicing self-awareness are certainly better prepared to cope with biases and their side effects.

---

[127] *Poème Sur La Loi Naturelle* (Editions La Bibliothèque Digitale, Paris, 1756), Quatrième Partie.

[128] Martie G. Haselton, Daniel Nettle, and Paul W. Andrews. "The Evolution of Cognitive Bias." *The Handbook of Evolutionary Psychology* (Hoboken, New Jersey, US: John Wiley & Sons Inc., 2005), Chapter 25, 724–746.

If you want an idea of how biased you are, you may take the Project Implicit test.[129] It is a free Harvard test that helps you to identify implicit biases. The key is not to think too much and answer questions quickly.

Let's take a look at some biases you're likely to encounter during negotiation:

RECIPROCITY

Reciprocity is a universal social rule. When we receive a gift, favor, or concession, we feel obliged to repay it (although we don't have to). We feel indebted to the giver. If repayment doesn't occur, we feel discomfort, remorse, or even fear of public shame. Favors and gifts are, therefore, never completely free, and the impulse to reciprocate can be quite powerful.

When you go to an Italian restaurant and the waiter offers you a free Limoncello before bringing you the bill, you're more likely to give a bigger tip. If your employer gives you gifts, you may surprise yourself working longer hours.

Reciprocity is ubiquitous in society, and is grounded upon the division of labor, exchange of goods and services, and other factors that contribute to our interdependence and need for cooperation.

You have probably noticed that the principle of reciprocity is often used in marketing. If you receive a free sample of a product, and you like the product, you might feel the need to reciprocate by buying the product. This is a classic tactic from marketers.

In the context of contract negotiations, reciprocity can come in the form of accepting an obligation or waiving a specific right on the understanding that the other party will be equally flexible. Sometimes I see a negotiator sticking rigidly to their ideal contract. Whereas a requested edit isn't threatening their position, and concession can give a level of comfort to the other party without risk. It is certainly important to stand your ground as a negotiator, but you shouldn't be close-fisted for the wrong reasons.

---

[129] https://implicit.harvard.edu/implicit/.

Reciprocity isn't always an instantaneous transaction. Often, a favor is offered with the understanding that the favored party will reciprocate when the opportunity arises. The person doing the favor may have no clear agenda. We will see later in this book the benefits of being a giver rather than a taker.

A golf invitation, concert tickets, free work, a useful introduction, and other favors can be offered with the secret objective of a return. However, gifts, favors, and concessions must be treated wisely. They can't be disproportionate. There's also often a thin line between a gift and a bribe. A difference in gender can also complicate things with a gift easily misinterpreted as an unprofessional overture or invitation.

Some corporations and governments have adopted rules regarding the giving and accepting of gifts and favors, but just about everyone is able to accept an invitation to a nice lunch. I personally don't hesitate to treat valuable contacts to a nice dinner or to offer them a nice bottle of wine with no end goal.

SELF-CONSISTENCY

Robert Cialdini gave a pertinent definition of a consistency bias in his book *Influence: The Psychology of Persuasion:* "*Once we have made a choice or taken a stand, we will encounter personal and interpersonal pressures to behave consistently with that commitment.*"[130] In other words, we like to comply to what we have previously said or done. We don't like to look inconsistent by changing our minds frequently in the eyes of others. We see it as a sign of weakness.

Politics shows us a clear example of this tendency. A candidate's every word is analyzed by experts and the media, and the most trifling inconsistency might be pointed out as "flip-flopping."

During negotiation, it is possible to encourage consistency in others and confront them later by asking the right questions in the right way. For instance, at the beginning of a meeting, you can mention that the goal of this negotiation is to reach a win-win outcome for all sides and make mutual

---

[130] Robert Cialdini, *Influence: The Psychology of Persuasion* (New York: Harper Collins, 2007), 57.

concessions in the interest of that outcome. If the other party agrees to this, you can remind them of this initial agreement when things get testy. There is a good chance that they will want to act in a manner consistent with their image of a compromising person.

Self-consistency doesn't mean that people will never breach their promises, but it will be harder for them to, especially if the commitment has been made without pressure and in public.

EGOCENTRISM

To me, this is one of the most difficult biases to overcome as a negotiator. We are inherently egocentric, and we tend to place ourselves at the center of the universe. We assess situations and people based on our own preferences and prejudices, and then we try to justify our actions rationally afterward. We also falsely assume that other people think like we do and share the same priorities.

Everyone sees the world in his own way. Dale Carnegie was probably right: *"people are not interested in you. They are not interested in me. They are interested in themselves – morning, noon and after dinner."*[131] In negotiation and elsewhere, egocentrism drives conflict, misunderstanding, and loss of opportunities. In 2014, Saint Louis University and the University of Amsterdam carried out a study. There were two groups of participants – one was assigned the role of unions, the other of employers. These groups were asked to negotiate a new labor agreement and discussed issues such as the number of paid vacation days and annual salary. After negotiating, participants were asked what they thought their opponents' expectations were. They were wrong on many occasions and lost opportunities for trade-offs. The authors provided an interesting insight of human nature:

> *"Whether it is because people simply know more about themselves than others and are more confident of what they know about themselves, or because self-knowledge comes to mind more easily, rapidly, and efficiently*

---

[131] Dale Carnegie, *How to Win Friends and Influence People*, Kindle, Loc. 865 of 3568.

than other knowledge, the self looms large in judgments that require people to take others into consideration, resulting in predictable judgment errors. People are thus 'egocentric' thinkers, having considerable difficulty casting aside their own unique perspective when attempting to take the perspective of another."[132]

Egocentrism manifests itself in many different ways. Here are some common ones:

- Self-serving: the tendency to take credit for success, while passing the blame for failure on others.
- Self-interest: the tendency to evaluate a situation or information in a way favorable to oneself.
- Win-lose syndrome: the tendency to believe that success for oneself comes at the expense of someone else.

Some egocentric attitudes are obvious. If you see someone who likes to be right, who exaggerates the truth to benefit themselves, who hogs the stage, who doesn't listen, who has an overcompetitive attitude, or who avoids taking responsibility when things go wrong, you're probably dealing with an egocentric person.

We don't like to be told that we're wrong, and we don't like to feel bad about ourselves. When someone triggers these feelings in us, our ego easily comes to our defense. If someone is egocentric by nature, they're likely to want to fight back in situations like these.

Self-awareness and mindfulness can help correct this bias. If you actively work on knowing yourself better while understanding and anticipating the priorities and interests of the other party in negotiation, you'll be less egocentric.

Negotiating with egocentric people is a challenge, especially if they're making little effort to understand your position. But it's possible to act in a way that can change the egocentric person's emotional state and make them

---

[132] John Chambers and Carsten De Dreu,. "Egocentrism Drives Misunderstanding in Conflict and Negotiation." *Journal of Experimental Social Psychology*, 51 (2014), 15-26.

more cooperative. The key is not to let your own ego get in the way.

When I organize exclusive dinners, I often deal with celebrity chefs. They are hugely talented, but some can be excessively demanding. They can behave as if the world revolves around them. They make little to no effort to adjust and trade-off. I've found that appreciation is an effective way to deal with them. I genuinely let them know what a fan I am of their work and show them gratitude for cooking for us. I sit on my ego so that things can run smoothly for the benefit of the events.

CONFORMITY AND ANALOGY

If someone doesn't have a strong opinion on a matter, their view will likely align with others around them.[133] Social conformism has a strong influence on decision-making. People align their views to those of others because they want to fit in. They often conform subconsciously. To many, the opinions of their peers are important.

As we mentioned earlier, social media is now used as a validation tool and is a good example of conformity in daily life. You're more likely to see (and like) something posted by one of your friends than by a stranger.

According to psychological scientist Daniel Haun, conformity helps keep society stable and starts at a very young age.[134] Although civilization has changed rapidly, we are still social animals following old rules that help us live a coordinated life together.

We have a great aptitude to think by analogy. We constantly identify similar things and associate them. It is mentally easy for us, helps us solve problems faster, and has contributed to many scientific discoveries. The problem is that analogical thinking can become an easy shortcut.

---

[133] Young Eun Huh, Joachim Vosgerau, and Carey K. Morewedge, "Social Defaults: Observed Choices Become Choice Defaults," *Journal of Consumer Research* 41, Issue 3 (October 2014): 746–760.

[134] Daniel B.M. Haun, Yvonne Rekers, and Michael Tomasello. "Children Conform to the Behavior of Peers; Other Great Apes Stick With What They Know." *Psychological Science* 25, no. 12 (December 2014): 2160–67.

Negotiators could have an interest in using the analogy bias to their advantage when appropriate. Something as simple as referring to competitors using your services or products can, for instance, make a difference at the time of convincing indecisive buyers.[135]

STATUS QUO BIAS

Most humans dislike change and are comfortable with their routines. Change introduces uncertainty, risk, additional work, liabilities, and so on. We often stick to the same brand, old plans, default choices, or anything that is comfortable. We are wired to take the path of least resistance.

When things are working fine, suggesting a change to someone is planting a dilemma in their mind. Their first intuition is often to say no and focus on prevention instead of promotion. To quote a famous saying, *"The devil you know is better than the devil you don't know."* Mild resistance to change is not necessarily bad, as it brings some form of stability in human relations and can encourage constructive criticism and brainstorming. However, it can also be completely irrational when a move would make perfect sense and explanations for inertia are vague or irrelevant.[136] Loss aversion is what often prevents people from changing.

NEGATIVITY BIAS

We pay more attention to bad news than good news. Our brain is more sensitive to negative information.[137] Negativity bias is Mother Nature arming us with threat detectors.

The problem is that we sometimes overestimate threats, and yet we also stress too much over small things. The same principle applies when we're

---

[135] Dedre Gentner. "Analogical reasoning, Psychology of." L. Nadel (editor), *Encyclopedia of Cognitive Science* (New York: Nature Publishing Group, 2003), 106-112.

[136] William Samuelson and Richard Zeckhauser, "Status Quo Bias in Decision Making," *Journal of Risk and Uncertainty*, (1988) 1: 7-59.

[137] Tiffany A. Ito, Jeff T. Larsen, Nancy K.R. Smith, and John T. Cacioppo. "Negative information weighs more heavily on the brain: the negativity bias in evaluative categorizations." *Journal of Personality and Social Psychology* 75, 4 (1998): 887-900.

watching the news as the bad news tends to stick in our minds more easily and longer than the good news.

In negotiation, this means that people tend to focus on the drawbacks of any potential deal, which could lead them to be overly cautious. To overcome the issue, greater attention should be given to the timing and way a proposal or idea is pitched. Like criticism, bad news should be sandwiched between layers of positivity, and the listener put in the right mood. That way, there is a better chance for the bad news to be well received.

The same way, your own brain can trick you as a negotiator, by giving too much importance to negative information. This could prevent you from seizing worthwhile opportunities. Stepping back and reassessing your risk should help you realign things. Be mindful of the true sources of your fears.

⌈19⌋ The Gender Impact

> With this genius peculiar to woman, who comprehends a man better than he does himself.
>
> —Victor Hugo[138]

Is negotiating with women different from negotiating with men? Our brains aren't much different. The male brain is on average bigger and contains a bit grayer matter in regions of the brain relating to intelligence. Women, on the other hand, have more white matter in the same area.

Gray matter corresponds to information processing whereas white matter corresponds to the networking of processing centers. According to scientists, it gives women an advantage in expressing and detecting emotions, as well as in language skills. This is why, until puberty, girls tend to be better with

---

[138] Victor Hugo, *Les Misérables* (Boston: Little Brown & Company, 1887), Chapter 10, 52.

language than boys.[139] Men seem to have an advantage in math and geometry, which requires local processing.[140]

It is true that women have an enhanced capacity for perception and are better able to spot the contradiction between a person's words and their body language. Experts consider women more intuitive than men and born with a better eye for close details.[141]

With a face sending more signals than any other part of the body, women have a better ability to detect these signals than men. For instance, it has been proven that women can better recognize happiness in facial expressions.[142] According to Allan and Barbara Pease, body language experts, this ability explains *"why few husbands can lie to their wives and get away with it and why, conversely, most women can pull the wool over a man's eyes without his realizing it."*[143]

Does this make women more emotionally intelligent? The answer may be a general yes, but there are indications that these differences tend to disappear at an executive level.[144] Because leaders must develop emotional intelligence in order to guide others effectively, it makes sense that these skills would develop in a comparable manner in anyone who has attained these top positions, regardless of gender.

Men are more active and competitive in negotiation than women. They initiate negotiation more often and also ask for what they want more often

---

[139] Douglas D. Burman, Tali Bitan, and James R. Booth, "Sex differences in neural processing of language among children," *Neuropsychologia* vol. 46 (2008): 1349-1362.

[140] Ann M. Gallagher and James C. Kaufman, *Gender Differences in Mathematics: An Integrative Psychological Approach* (Cambridge: Cambridge University Press, 2005).

[141] James Owen, "Men and Women Really Do See Things Differently", *National Geographic News*, September 6, 2012

[142] Uta-Susan Donges, Anette Kersting, and Thomas Suslow (2012), "Women's Greater Ability to Perceive Happy Facial Emotion Automatically: Gender Differences in Affective Priming," PLoS ONE 7(7): e41745.

[143] Allan and Barbara Pease, *The Definitive Book on Body Language* (New York: Bantam Dell, 2004), 13.

[144] Business Wire, "Women Poised to Effectively Lead in Matrix Work Environments, Hay Group Research Finds," March 27, 2012.

than women do. This is a cultural and social norm in many countries. When a man is assertive in negotiation, he might be identified as a go-getter. If a woman behaves the same way in similar circumstances, she might be pegged as demanding, bossy, or breaching social norms. This makes people less inclined to cooperate with her, and she will act less assertively to avoid social consequences.

Men generally achieve better results at negotiation than women. This doesn't have anything to do with competence or ability.[145] On the contrary, stereotypes, social pressure, and fear of backlash for women impacts these outcomes.[146] Women are often unfairly perceived as being weaker, less competent, and more easily misled than men. When negotiating, men tend to be more deceptive with women than they are with other men.[147] This is because many men tend to consider women less capable and try to use this stereotype to their advantage. It has been proven that men will more easily hide information from women but share the same information with men in similar situations.[148]

Negotiation is also often viewed as a "masculine thing." This perception presents a number of obstacles for women. Women who believe in this stereotype may feel that they're not entitled to behave in ways that might be to their advantage at the negotiating table. For fear of seeming "difficult," they might set low expectations for their performance and achieve a lackluster outcome. Ginni Rometty, CEO of IBM, was interviewed at the FORTUNE Most

---

[145] Charles B. Craver and David W. Barnes, "Gender, Risk Taking, and Negotiation Performance," *Michigan Journal of Gender and Law*, 1999, 5:2, 298-352.

[146] Emily T. Amanatullah and Michael W. Morris, "Negotiating gender roles: gender differences in assertive negotiating are mediated by women's fear of backlash and attenuated when negotiating on behalf of others," *Journal of Personality and Social Psychology* (2010) 98:2, 256-267.

[147] Laura J. Kray, Jessica Ashley Kennedy, and Alex B. Van Zant, "Not Competent Enough to Know the Difference? Gender Stereotypes About Women's Ease of Being Misled Predict Negotiator Deception," *Organizational Behavior and Human Decision Processes*, 125(2) (2014).

[148] Nolan Feeney, "Study: Women More Likely to Be Lied to in Negotiations Than Men," *Time*, August 3, 2014.

Powerful Women Summit on October 5, 2011. She gave an eloquent example of this obstacle facing women in the workplace. She was once offered a great management position, but, doubtful of her own abilities, she asked for more time to think the position over. When she was at dinner with her husband that evening, she told him what had happened, and her husband replied, *"Do you think a man ever answers a question that way?"*[149]

Women tend to pay higher prices for the same product or service than men and are offered lower salaries because they bargain less, even for high-paying positions. This could be one of the many factors contributing to the gender pay gap. Top male executives still earn millions more than women who hold similar positions.[150,151]

Yet women who manage to overcome these social pressures and backlash often achieve great outcomes and turn out to be remarkable negotiators. The successful, high-profile women I've known in the business world have overcome disadvantages to become more assertive, demanding with themselves, and resilient. Many have had to prove themselves and affirm their abilities in a climate that tends to negate or ignore them. Like tea bags, they have shown how strong they are when they got into hot water. Barbara Corcoran, real estate guru and cohost of *Shark Tank*, is a good example of what a skilled and successful woman negotiator can accomplish. Having said this, I have always found women in the Eastern world better appreciated for their true worth compared to women in the Western world. Asian women are often the ones holding the purse strings and the true decision makers or influencers in business.

If men perform better at negotiation, women generally perform better than men at negotiating or advocating for others (whether an individual or a

---

[149] "IBM's Ginni Rometty on taking risks," YouTube video, 3:01, "Fortune Magazine," October 25, 2011, https://www.youtube.com/watch?v=Du_aOCCJkWE/.

[150] Julia Carpenter, "The gender pay gap doesn't close – even at the very, very top," *CNN Business Online*, December 13, 2017.

[151] Julia Carpenter, "In high-paying jobs, the wage gap can cost women millions," *CNN Business Online*, December 19, 2018.

group). This is probably in part because they can make greater demands on behalf of others than for themselves. In addition, women may feel like they don't have to comply as rigidly to stereotypes when they're not perceived as negotiating on their own behalf.[152]

Men will take more risks than women, particularly financial ones[153]. This principle also applies when individuals are under stress. An interesting study from 2012 shows that *"stress amplifies gender differences in strategies during risky decisions, with males taking more risk and females less risk under stress. These gender differences in behavior are associated with differences in activity in the insula and dorsal striatum, brain regions involved in computing risk and preparing to take action."*[154]

Contrary to the common idea than women are chattier in group discussions and meetings, men are generally more talkative than women and hold the floor more often.[155] Men also tend to use more nonverbal communication, whether consciously or not, which gives a better indication of their internal state. Women are more observant than men; they listen more and smile more.[156] They will generally spend more time than men observing cues.

What about charm? Do women have an advantage in negotiation?

As early as 1716, François de Callières noticed the danger of succumbing to the siren song:

---

[152] Emily T. Amanatullah and Michael W. Morris, "Negotiating gender roles: Gender differences in assertive negotiating are mediated by women's fear of backlash and attenuated when negotiating on behalf of others," *Journal of Personality and Social Psychology*, 98(2), Feb. 2010, 256-267.

[153] Gary Charness and Uri Gneezy, "Strong Evidence for Gender Differences in Risk Taking," *Journal of Economic Behavior & Organization*, 83 (2012): 50–58.

[154] Mara Mather and Nichole R. Lighthall, "Both Risk and Reward are Processed Differently in Decisions Made Under Stress," *Current Directions in Psychological Science*, 21(2) Feb. 2012, 36-41.

[155] Shari Kendall and Deborah Tannen, "Gender and Language in the Workplace," from *Gender and Discourse*, edited by Ruth Wodak. (London: SAGE Publications, 1997), 81-105.

[156] Agneta Fisher and Marianne LaFrance. "What Drives the Smile and the Tear: Why Women are More Emotionally Expressive Than Men," *Emotion Review*, 7(1) 2015, 22-29.

It is well-known that the power of feminine charm often extends to cover the weightiest resolution of state [...] but a negotiator must never forget that love's companions are indiscretion and imprudence, and that moment he becomes pledged to the whim of a favored woman, no matter how wise he may be, he runs the grave risk of being no longer master of his own secrets.[157]

The danger is scientifically proven. Men, especially young ones, will take greater risks and act more irrationally in the presence of an attractive woman as their testosterone level elevates.[158] There's also evidence that flirtatious women can achieve better outcomes in negotiation.[159]

Is charm an effective strategy for women then? It can work, but it has its limits. This charm must be, to the highest extent possible, authentic, subtle, and remain professional in order for the desired impact to be achieved. Otherwise, it can work against a woman's goals and defeat the purpose she has in mind.

In a community of mostly men, displaying signs of femininity can be distracting, even alluring, but in a business context, more masculine expressions in women, such as a firm handshake or understated clothing, may work to their advantage, as it may make them appear more credible.

Madeleine Albright, American politician and diplomat, when interviewed by Bill Maher in 2009, admitted to having used charm in negotiation.[160] She also said, *"I think women are really good at making friends and not good at*

---

[157] François de Callières, *On the Manner of Negotiating with Princes* (New York: Houghton Mifflin, 2000), 15.

[158] Richard Ronay and William von Hippel. "The Presence of an Attractive Woman Elevates Testosterone and Physical Risk Taking in Young Men," *Social Psychological and Personality Science* 1, no. 1 (January 2010): 57–64.

[159] Laura J. Kray, Connson C. Locke, and Alex B. Van Zant. "Feminine charm: an experimental analysis of its costs and benefits in negotiations," *Personality & Social Psychology Bulletin* 38 10 (2012): XX(X) 1-15.

[160] Bill Maher. 2009. "March 20, 2009." *Real Time with Bill Maher*. HBO. https://www.huffpost.com/entry/flirting-with-negotiation_b_2094668

networking. Men are good at networking and not necessarily making friends. That's a gross generalization, but I think it holds in many ways."[161]

[20] The Group Effect

Don't let the noise of others' opinions drown out your own inner voice.

—Steve Jobs[162]

Negotiating one-on-one is not the same as negotiating with or as part of a group. Being part of a group can positively or negatively impact your own performance. A pooling of resources and talents can help everyone involved reach higher objectives. However, group discussions and negotiation can present some adverse effects that readers should be aware of.

One risk is the concept of group polarization, which is well documented. Group polarization happens when a group makes more extreme decisions than its individual members would be inclined to support. This is especially true when responsibility for decisions isn't placed in a leader's hands, and deliberation takes place among the group's members. Suppose an executive is supporting an important change of strategy within the company he works for. He may end up supporting it more vigorously during group deliberation. This same principle might lead an individual who is typically less decisive to adopt a more assertive attitude when bolstered by the support of a group. In both cases, critical thinking and a careful consideration of adverse effects of a decision are put on the back burner.

Polish psychologist Solomon Asch was deeply interested in group polarization. He conducted an experiment in which he assembled a group of 7 to 9

---

[161] "Madeleine Albright on Barriers Broken and Barriers that Remain," *Wall Street Journal*, May 7, 2012

[162] "Steve Jobs' 2005 Stanford Commencement Address," YouTube video, 15:04, "Stanford," March 7, 2008, https://www.youtube.com/watch?v=UF8uR6Z6KLc/.

people. All but one had met previously with the experimenter, and those who had were instructed to respond on certain trials with wrong and unanimous judgments. One person in the group was not aware of the prearrangement. 2 cards were placed in front of the participants. One card had a vertical line on it (standard line), and the other had three other lines for comparison. Participants were all asked to match the length of the standard line with one of the 3 other lines in a public manner, the only true participant being asked last. One third of the time, the true participant conformed to the majority view, even though he knew it was wrong.[163]

Multiple factors explain the polarization phenomenon: social influences and pressure, conformism, fear of appearing weak in the eyes of others, efforts to be accepted by a cohesive group, reluctance to challenge established group rules, and more.[164]

Polarization can be present at many levels of a society, from board meetings to juries, and it has led to many bad decisions. Social media platforms have made the phenomenon even more widespread. Online conversations on sensitive matters such as abortion, gun control, racism, just to name a few, provide good examples of extreme positions taken by group members.

The risk of group polarization tends to diminish when a group is led by one decision maker, but when there's an assembly of parties of equal power, the risk increases. It also increases with strong bargaining conditions or heated debates.

"Groupthink" is also the term coined by psychologist Irving Janis to describe this phenomenon. More specifically, Janis refers to *"a mode of thinking that persons engage in when concurrence thinking becomes so dominant in a cohesive group that it tends to override realistic appraisal of alternative*

---

[163] Solomon Asch, "Studies of Independence and Conformity: I. A Minority of One Against a Unanimous Majority," *Psychological Monographs: General and Applied*, 70(9), 1956, 1-70.

[164] Cass R. Sunstein, "The Law of Group Polarization" (December 1999). University of Chicago Law School, *John M. Olin Law & Economics Working Paper* No. 91.

courses of action."[165] Janis analyzed a few extreme historical decisions made by a group, such as the choice made by the United States to secretly invade Cuba in 1961, with the help of Cuban opponents. The operation was a complete fiasco and led to the Cuban Missile Crisis. The world was close to a third world war. Men involved in the decision to invade the Bay of Pigs were far from stupid (starting with John Fitzgerald Kennedy). According to Janis, they were probably all victims of groupthink. Despite the riskiness of the operation, they failed to question the feasibility of an invasion and disregarded the consequences, possibly to avoid internal conflict. Stress and fear may also have played important roles.

Another challenge for negotiators is group dynamics. Moods and emotions play an important role in negotiation and can be contagious. The mood of a group's leader transfers to its members. Groups led by those with a positive attitude tend to perform better.[166] Therefore, the leader of a group should be, to the highest extent possible, identified and observed as they set the pace of negotiation and influence the attitudes of others.

Groups can fall prey to emotions just like people do. Their members can share enthusiasm or anxiety. This is called "group affective tone" and has an impact on team performance.[167] When you're leading a team, try spreading positive energy and appreciation. Chances are, you'll face more cooperation and less resistance within the group.

Each group dynamic is different, and, when possible, it's helpful to determine how tasks are divided, who makes the decisions, which members are most influential, and what rivalries might exist or arise. If you develop an eye for group dynamics, you may be able to influence some members of a group

---

[165] Irving L. Janis, *Leadership: Understanding the Dynamics of Power and Influence in Organizations* (Indiana, US: University of Notre Dame Press, 2007), 157.

[166] Thomas Sy, Stéphane Côté, and Richard Saavedra (2005). "The Contagious Leader: Impact of the Leader's Mood on the Mood of Group Members, Group Affective Tone, and Group Processes," *Journal of Applied Psychology*, 90(2), 295-305.

[167] Hilko Frederik Klaas Paulsen, Florian Erik Klonek, Kurt Schneider, and Simone Kauffeld, "Group Affective Tone and Team Performance: A Week-Level Study in Project Teams," *Frontiers in Communication*, November 10, 2016.

to serve your interests. And if you are part of a group of negotiators, it goes without saying that you should be scrupulously aware of the characteristics of your group, especially if you are the leader. A team with a blinded leader can be well on its way to self-sabotage.

When you're working in a group, you may have noticed that some individuals work less hard than others. This is what social scientists call "social loafing." It is officially defined as *"a decrease in individual effort due to the social presence of other persons."*[168]

An article in the *Journal of Personality and Social Psychology* provides a list of reasons people might lower their efforts within a group: *"Individuals are more likely to engage in social loafing when their individual outputs cannot be evaluated collectively, when working on tasks that are perceived as low in meaningfulness or personal involvement, when a group-level comparison standard is not available, when working with strangers, when they expect their co-workers to perform well, and when their inputs to the collective outcome are redundant with those of other group members."*[169]

Forewarned is forearmed. If you lead a group of negotiators, especially if they are involved in a protracted and labor-intensive negotiation, it is important you keep all contributors on alert and committed for better cohesion and performance.

There are two other important aspects of group negotiation that negotiators should consider. When different groups of people are negotiating against each other, things usually get more complicated. This is because a feeling of competition between them is triggered, causing a decrease in cooperation. Whenever possible, try to limit the number of participants in a negotiation to avoid such complexity and eliminate the presence of those who are not crucial to the negotiation.

---

[168] Bibb Latané, Kipling Williams, and Stephen Harkins, "Many Hands Make Light the Work: The Causes and Consequences of Social Loafing," *Journal of Personality and Social Psychology*, 1979, 37(6), 822-832.

[169] Steven J. Karau and Kipling D. Williams, "Social loafing: A meta-analytic review and theoretical integration," *Journal of Personality and Social Psychology*, 1993. 65(4), 681-706.

Because a group generally has more intellectual resources than a single person, an individual negotiator can easily be outperformed. If you're going to be in such a situation, you should know that it requires extra preparation. You should prepare, leaving no stone unturned. Your mind should be sharp, organized, and focused.

[21] The Status Motivator

> Apart from economic payoffs, social status seems to be the most important incentive and motivating force of social behavior.
>
> —John Harsanyi[170]

Across cultures, people pay great attention to status, which can be conferred on the basis of age, gender, descendance, education, occupation, and income, to name a few. Hierarchy instills order, helps to secure resources, and supposedly brings growth. It also creates inequalities that, though often unjust, are generally accepted because it provides some kind of stability. There are two ways to gain status in this world: competition with others or cooperation with others.

In modern societies, the more capable are elevated. Stories of social success are valued and told. Bonuses, promotions, and offers are dangled in front of those who would work to achieve them.

In the United States, the act of climbing the social ladder has long been idealized and promoted. In countries like India, where hierarchies are more rigid, a category of people seek to maintain their existing social gains and discourage others from moving upward.

Our well-being and self-esteem are largely derived from what people think of us, whether we're willing to admit it or not. We like to feel liked,

---

[170] John C. Harsanyi, *Essays on Ethics, Social Behaviour, and Scientific Explanation* (Dordrecht, Holland: Reidel Publishing Company, 1976), 204.

recognized, and important. Many of us feel happier if we are better off than our neighbors or have a bigger house. It is also proven that money makes us happy if it improves our social ranking. Income alone does not.[171]

In this context, the desire to increase or maintain social status can lead negotiators to follow their personal interests and forget about their initial objective. Most negotiators, consciously or unconsciously, hope a good negotiation outcome will elevate their status. Greater status, especially within a corporation, can lead to the perception of greater value. Many are also tempted to help themselves at the expense of their employer. However, when a negotiator's personal and professional goals aren't compatible, outcomes suffer. I've seen negotiators make deals simply to put a notch in their belt, trapping their company in an expensive contract. Those who take this approach play the short-term game.

Negotiation is often a scene for social inequality, which can have a significant impact on its results. People of different status facing each other in negotiation tend to approach it in a more competitive and conflictual manner.[172] Unsatisfied negotiators may feel, consciously or unconsciously, frustration, resentment, and even jealousy toward those who hold privilege. Reversely, the privileged may display a sense of contempt or arrogance, sometimes without even realizing it. This is why labor union negotiations are often the toughest ones. Wages, hours, and working conditions are at the center of the discussions, but concessions are difficult to extract because of an underlying class struggle taking place.

Whatever your status as a negotiator, always strive to be respectful of others whatever their status. Acknowledge them, and express appreciation for their work, time, or efforts. Don't lose focus on what really matters. Keep in mind that the conditions in which people grow and live impact the way they

---

[171] C. J. Boyce,, G. D. A. Brown, and S. C. Moore (2010), "Money and Happiness: Rank of Income, Not Income, Affects Life Satisfaction," *Psychological Science*, 21(4), 471–475.

[172] Lindred Greer and Corinne Bendersky. "Power and Status in Conflict and Negotiation Research: Introduction to the Special Issue." November 2013, *Negotiation and Conflict Management Research*, 6(4) 239–252.

[22] Why Integrity Pays Better

> Thus, we have on stage two men, each of whom knows nothing of what he believes the other knows, and to deceive each other reciprocally both speak in allusions, each of the two hoping (in vain) that the other holds the key to his puzzle.
>
> —Umberto Eco[173]

There is a good chance that you'll get played at negotiation. 27 to 100 percent of any negotiation would be tainted with deception (such as lies, exaggeration, denigration, omission, or denial) according to social studies and depending on the context and consequences for such behavior.[174,175] Almost every one of us has likely been deceptive when negotiating. For some, it is a legitimate strategy, and for others it is unethical.

Research identifies the main factors driving deception in negotiation: greed, competition, fear, uncertainty, envy, and experienced injustice.[176,177] The lure of power, money, and benefits, as well as the need to protect our

---

[173] Umberto Eco, *The Island of the Day Before* (New York: Harcourt Brace & Company, 1994), 399.

[174] Karl Aquino and Thomas Becker. "Lying in negotiations: How individual and situational factors influence the use of neutralization strategies." *Journal of Organizational Behavior*, 2005, 26(6). 661-679.

[175] Lyn Van Swol, Deepak Malhotra, and Michael T. Braun, "Deception and Its Detection: Effects of Monetary Incentives and Personal Relationship History." *Communication Research*, 2010, XX (X), 1-22.

[176] Francesca Gino and Catherine Shea, "Deception in Negotiations: The Role of Emotions," in *The Oxford Handbook of Economic Conflict Resolution*, edited by G. E. Bolton and R. T. A. Croson (Oxford: Oxford University Press, Inc., 2012), 47-60.

[177] S. Moran and M. E. Schweitzer (2008). "When Better Is Worse: Envy and the Use of Deception." *Negotiation and Conflict Management Research*, 1 (1), 3-29.

interests, lead us to lie by commission (we misrepresent information) or omission (we decide not to reveal important information). But we are more reticent to lie by commission than by omission, as a lie by commission makes us feel guiltier.

History provide great examples of famous lies by omission or commission. We all remember the infamous moment when Bill Clinton, president of the United States of America, addressed the American people with these words: "*I am going to say this again. I did not have sexual relations with that woman.*"

In 1919, an Italian immigrant convinced thousands in New England to invest in a postage coupon, promising a 50 percent return in 45 days and 100 percent in 90 days. Fresh money invested was used to pay early investors and so on. The equivalent of USD $225 million was defrauded. His name was Charles Ponzi, and the Ponzi scheme was named after him. Almost a century later, Bernie Madoff would be arrested for running a similar scam.

The business world is littered with examples of unethical practices. Enron, Lehman Brothers, and Arthur Andersen are just a few of the organizations whose very names call up associations of greed, dishonesty, and illegal actions. Although these can be seen as extreme cases, it is true that deception remains part of human nature.

Our ability to cooperate can also function as an ability to manipulate. Long ago, competition over women, food, and other necessities birthed this seemingly necessary evil. According to Allan and Barbara Pease, *"if you told everyone the complete truth all the time, you'd not only end up lonely, you might even end up in hospital or in prison. Lying is the oil that greases our interactions with others."*[178] It is probably true.

Because so many negotiators see negotiation as a winning exercise, it's not surprising that deceptive tactics are common in negotiation. Someone with the win-lose mentality, who views negotiation as competition, will be more likely to use deceptive tactics. Those who view negotiation in terms of cooperation won't feel the need to employ these devices as often.

---

[178] Allan and Barbara Pease, *The Definitive Book on Body Language* (New York: Bantam Dell, 2004), 143.

The more power you have, the more tempting it is to use deception in negotiation because you feel more entitled. Donald Trump may have been even more misleading as a president than he was as a businessman. In July and August 2018, it is reported that he would have averaged the astonishing number of 16 false claims a day.[179] Donald Trump actually advocates deceptive behaviors in his book *The Art of the Deal*. He calls it "truthful hyperbole" and defines it as *"an innocent form of exaggeration – and a very effective form of promotion."*[180]

People who want to access power also tend to be more deceptive. Their motive, generally, is that they want to sound more likable or make an impression.[181] This may be the reason for a majority of people to inflate their resume, hoping to get a job and reach a certain position. Interestingly, most people consider themselves ethical. If they use deceptive tactics, they find a good explanation for their decision such as a necessity to defend themselves, or to reciprocate the deceptive tactics of the other party, who started it first, of course.

As men are more competitive in negotiation than women, it is not surprising to hear that men have also been shown to be more deceptive than women in this arena. This has been corroborated by several studies. Among the most well-known of these is that of Leigh Thompson, professor at the Kellogg School of Management, who brought two people into a lab and placed them in different rooms. One participant was given an envelope to split with the other. 44 percent of the male participants misrepresented the amount available to the other participants, whereas 29 percent of women did the same.[182]

---

[179] Susan B. Glasser, "It's True: Trump Is Lying More, and He's Doing It on Purpose," *The New Yorker*, August 3, 2018.

[180] David Barstow, "Donald Trump's Deals Rely on Being Creative With the Truth," *The New York Times,* July 16, 2016.

[181] Robert S. Feldman, James A. Forrest, and Benjamin R. Happ, "Self-Presentation and Verbal Deception: Do Self-Presenters Lie More?" *Basic and Applied Social Psychology*, 2002, 24(2), 163–170.

[182] Leigh Thompson, "Research: Simple Prompts Can Get Women to Negotiate More Like Men, and Vice Versa," *Harvard Business Review*, September 17, 2018.

Men are apparently even more deceptive when women are present at the bargaining table.[183] Having said this, the women who do lie tend to be better at it than their male colleagues. This is likely due to their greater intuitive capacity. They generally perceive nonverbal cues better and therefore can fake them better. Their lies can be subtler and more sophisticated than those of men.

Naturally, the higher the incentives, the greater the risk of deceptive behavior. When there's a world to gain or lose, otherwise scrupulous people can go to extremes. We all agree that a negotiator cannot be an open book, and lies, especially those by omission, are in a way part of the equation. Information can be strategic or confidential and may require a high level of trust to be shared. Having said that, honesty pays off better overall. Honest people are more successful at doing business in the long run. They maintain authenticity, keep their word, and have better reputations. They gain more respect and in turn attract more opportunities. I think no one has summarized it better than François de Callières again:

> *The good negotiator, moreover, will never find the success of his mission on promises which he cannot redeem or on bad faith. It is a capital error, which prevails widely, that a clever negotiator must be a master of the art of deceit. Deceit indeed is but a measure of the smallness of mind of him who employs it, and simply shows that his intelligence is too meagerly equipped to enable him to arrive at his ends by just and reasonable methods. No doubt the art of lying has been practiced with success in diplomacy; but unlike that honesty, which is the best policy, a lie always leaves a drop of poison behind, and even the most dazzling diplomatic success gained by dishonesty stands on an insecure foundation, for it awakes in the defeated party a sense of aggravation, a desire of vengeance, and a hatred which must always be a menace for his foe.*[184]

---

[183] Jussi Palomäki, Jeff Yan, David Modic, and Michael Laakasuo, "'To Bluff like a Man or Fold like a Girl?' – Gender Biased Deceptive Behavior in Online Poker," (2016), PLOS ONE 11(7).

[184] François de Callières, *On the Manner of Negotiating with Princes* (New York: Houghton Mifflin, 2000), 21.

One classic technique to spot a liar is to identify contradictions in their words or reasoning. In my experience, liars with bad memories are often the easiest to pick out, while creative people tend to be the most difficult. You have to ask questions that are open-ended and pertinent to invite them to disclose more information. The more data you get, the easier it will be to detect holes in reasoning. Questions should be rather direct, as people lie less often when asked specifically. For instance, the seller of a secondhand car, knowing that his car has a technical issue that does not need immediate attention, will be less inclined to lie to his buyer if this buyer specifically asked him about it. The seller will be less comfortable to lie by commission.[185]

Liars tend to be slower to answer. They take longer pauses and are more hesitant and evasive. They tend to use more words to justify themselves. They use fewer first-person pronouns in order to distance themselves from the lie. They use more words that convey negative emotions, like "afraid," difficult," "limited," "poor," "mess," and others.[186,187]

Many of the cues necessary to detect liars are nonverbal. The challenge consists of spotting inconsistencies between the liar's words and their gestures. When someone lies, it usually provokes a detectable physical reaction. People start touching their faces. This is because liars often experience an increase in brain activity during deception. They're thinking about what they said or didn't say and are anxious about getting caught. Touching their face is their attempt to calm themselves. They may also gulp, blink more often, or avoid eye contact. Bill Clinton famously touched his nose when he was asked

---

[185] Maurice E. Schweitzer and Rachel Croson, "Curtailing deception: The impact of direct questions on lies and omissions," *International Journal of Conflict Management*; July 1999; 10(3): 225-248.

[186] Jason Dou, Michelle Liu, Haaris Muneer, and Adam Schlussel, "What Words Do We Use to Lie? Word Choice in Deceptive Messages," Cornell University, 2017.

[187] Matthew L. Newman, James W. Pennebaker, Diane S. Berry, and Jane M. Richards, "Lying Words: Predicting Deception from Linguistic Styles," *Personality and Social Psychology Bulletin, 29(5), May 2003: 665-675.*

if he and Monica Lewinsky had had an affair.[188]

People also tend to smile less when they're lying. This is due to the fact that smiling is interpreted as a sign of lying. When liars try to smile, their smile usually looks fake. Deception is and will always be present in negotiation, but it should not be used as a general tactic. Ability to detect deceptive behaviors and seek truth in others should be mastered instead. This isn't an easy skill to learn. One must be a good listener and observant. According to research, only 54 percent of us are able to detect a liar.[189]

[23] The Risk Factor

> Whenever two parties come together to transact business of any kind, one side is always asking the other (consciously or otherwise) to assume more or all of the risk. If you ask someone to take all the risk, their first inclination is not to buy.
>
> —Jay Abraham[190]

Most people are risk sensitive, especially when they are pushed to make a choice and money is involved. This sensitivity is fueled by the attention we develop for negative aspects of things and bad news. The feeling of pain is also greater than the pleasure of gain.

If given a chance at an opportunity with a high potential payoff but an uncertain outcome, most will choose to stay home. In a study carried out in 2000, *twelve subjects worked on a decision-making task with two alternatives: (a) a small reward at a high probability of reinforcement (non-risky option), and*

---

[188] Martin Grunwald, Thomas Weiss, Stephanie R. Mueller, and Lysann Rall. "EEG changes caused by spontaneous facial self-touch may represent emotion regulating processes and working memory maintenance." *Brain Research* 1557 (2014): 111-126.

[189] Charles F. Bond, Jr., and Bella M. DePaulo, "Accuracy of Deception Judgments." *Personality and Social Psychology Review* 10(3) (2006): 214–234.

[190] Jay Abraham, *Getting Everything You Can Out of All You've Got* (New York: St. Martin's Press, 2000), 21.

(b) a larger reward at a much smaller reinforcement probability (risky option), All but one subject showed a strong preference for the non-risky alternative.[191]

Of course, some of us are perennial risk takers. Mark Zuckerberg is one of them. He thinks that *"In a world of change, the bigger risk is not taking any risk."*[192] Mark Zuckerberg's case is an exception, though. I'm not saying that we don't or shouldn't take risks in life, but, in general, human beings avoid risk. In turn, negotiations often fail because a party feels that they're being exposed to too much risk. Therefore, one of your missions as a negotiator is to clear away as much risk as possible and offer comfort to the people you negotiate with. For instance, you can offer some warranties to your counterpart, show supportive facts, clarify your reputation, or even develop further rapport.

If people trust you, they will be more willing to take risks. While setting up a wine fund in 2011, I had to tour to raise money. Wine is an alternative asset, and many people are unfamiliar with it. Investors weren't easy to convince. In the end, those who took the risk were the ones who trusted me and saw me as a credible person. They'd come to my dinners and see me associated with authorities in the industry. They'd see me investing my own money in the fund and would be convinced by the true performance of wine as an asset class in the past twenty years.

You should learn to detect risk-taking persons, but it's important to remember that people may take risks in one domain but not another. Just because you drive over the speed limit doesn't mean that you're prepared to take financial risks.

Emotions such as anger or joy usually push people to take more risks. Lack of self-control makes people more daring as well.[193] Some negotiators work to trigger these emotions in others for just this reason.

---

[191] Scott D. Lane and Don R. Cherek. "Risk Aversion in Human Subjects Under Conditions of Probabilistic Reward." *The Psychological Record* (2000), 50, 221-234.

[192] "Mark Zuckerberg: How to Build the Future," YouTube Video, 25:26, "Y Combinator" August 16, 2016. https://www.youtube.com/watch?v=Lb4IcGF5iTQ/.

[193] Nicholas Freeman and Mark Muraven. "Self-Control Depletion Leads to Increased Risk Taking," *Social Psychological and Personality Science*, Vol. 1(2), 175-181.

⌈IN ESSENCE⌉

- *Human action can be modified to some extent, but human nature cannot be changed.*
- Humans base their decisions more on what they see than on what they hear.
- Pay great attention to the signals you send and that are sent to you. Do not overfocus on your words and don't let your emotions impair your judgment.
- Develop a catalogue of human signals and expressions and practice reading. Human communication is mostly nonverbal.
- Be assertive when necessary but always do it with composure.
- Fear can break your focus and direct your attention to a disproportionate concern for the consequences of your actions. Learn to understand and control your fears.
- Anger is the most dangerous of all emotions. Don't let your emotions make your decisions.
- *Keep calm and watch out for your first reaction. It may be you at your worst, not at your best.*
- We can't analyze every phenomenon we perceive, so our minds take mental shortcuts.
- Be aware that most biases escape our conscious notice and can have a significant impact on our behavior.
- Women are more intuitive than men and born with a better eye for detail. They have a better ability to detect facial expressions than men.
- Group polarization and groupthink can cloud critical thinking and require a careful consideration of adverse effects.
- Because a group of negotiators generally has more intellectual resources than a single person, an individual negotiator facing it can easily be outperformed. Be extra prepared.

- Our well-being and self-esteem are largely derived from what people think of us, whether we're willing to admit it or not. We like to feel liked, recognized, and important.
- The desire to increase or maintain social status can lead negotiators to follow their personal interests and forget about their initial objective.
- There is a good chance that you'll get played at negotiation. Lies can dangerously affect your reputation and credibility. Sooner or later, you have to sit down to a banquet of consequences.
- Honest people are more successful at doing business in the long run. They maintain authenticity, keep their word, and better their reputation. They gain respect this way and in turn attract more opportunities.
- Only 54 percent of us are able to detect a liar.
- Most people are risk sensitive, especially when they are pushed to make a choice and money is involved.
- Clear most risk away from the bargaining table and offer comfort to the people you negotiate with for better outcomes.

CHAPTER FIVE:

Influencing Others

The secret of my influence has always been that it remains secret.

—Salvador Dali[194]

The ability to influence others is key in negotiation. It requires a good understanding of human psychology and the overcoming of a number of pitfalls. Influencing others does not consist of winning a debate of ideas or proving the superiority of an intellect. Rather influence is gained by subtly making people like you and finally trust you, so you can affect their decisions with your ideas. Influence combines power and warmth toward others.

Key influencers rule this world. They are the ones we like for their authenticity, their ideas, their personality, and their authority. They are the ones we chase and follow on media. They get what they want more easily than others because they have perfected the art. And this art can be learned.

---

[194] Salvador Dali, *The Secret Life of Salvador Dali* (New York: Dover Publications Inc, 1993), 315.

[24] Build Rapport

> The ability to establish rapport is one of the most important skills a person can have. To be a good performer or a good salesman, a good parent or a good friend, a good persuader or a good politician, what you really need is a rapport, the ability to form a powerful common human bond.
>
> —Tony Robbins[195]

Negotiation truly starts by building rapport with others and before discussing any terms of an agreement. Rapport fosters cooperation and concessions because the negotiators on both sides are more likely to see and seek common ground when bonding.

Tony Robbins defines it as a "total responsiveness between two people" and "the ability to enter someone else's world."[196] When rapport takes place, conflict and differences are reduced. Good feelings and trust are heightened and communication is made easy.

It is important to understand that rapport is a precondition to trust. It is to no one's benefit to readily trust a stranger. Rather, trust is something that is established and earned through rapport.

We give more trust to people who are alike and with whom we share interests, personality traits, or even appearance. Character similarity produces the comfort of the familiar, the understood, the trusted. An insincere, inauthentic, or one-sided rapport creates the risk of seeing the relationship quickly fading and defenses rising.

The best public speakers know how to build great rapport with their audiences. They choose their words carefully, they are in control of their

---

[195] Tony Robbins, *Unlimited Power: The New Science of Personal Achievement* (New York: Simon & Schuster Paperbacks, 1986), 231.

[196] Tony Robbins, *Unlimited Power: The New Science of Personal Achievement* (New York, Simon & Schuster Paperbacks, 2015), 230.

own body language, they smile, eventually use humor or empathy to relax the audience, focus on the assembly's values, etc. These levels of engagement break down barriers of resistance and open people to be more receptive to their ideas. David Brooks, author of *The Social Animal*, concurs with this opinion when he considers that *"politicians do have incredible social skills. When you meet them, they lock into you, they look you in the eye, they invade your personal space, they massage the back of your head."*[197]

Bill Clinton is a master of building rapport and influencing people. He is known for giving full attention to people he talks to. He is present, listens well, and connects with each person with whom he speaks. Eye contact is key in Bill Clinton's interpersonal communication skills. He is also a warm and tactile person.[198]

The reality of the modern age makes it increasingly difficult to sell things face-to-face to people, including ideas. We are constantly sought out to buy products and services, there is noise and distraction everywhere, and we end up on the defensive just to think clearly. Do you remember the time when telemarketing was a powerful selling tool and we had time to answer people on the phone? This time is gone and now we cut these conversations short for lack of time and distrust.

Unless you have a very strong brand and unique product or service that people want or need now, rapport is more necessary than ever to build a relationship and gain trust.

How do you build a genuine rapport that produces the expected benefits? Often people think that the best way to establish a relationship and convince people is through words. In reality, focusing on establishing a conversation first is not the most efficient way to begin building rapport. Rather, listening closely and observing your counterpart enables a faster route to establish it.

---

[197] David Brooks, "The Social Animal," TED2011, March 2011, 18:29, https://www.ted.com/talks/david_brooks_the_social_animal?/.

[198] "Bill Clinton Has a Superpower, and Mastering It Can Make You Successful Beyond Belief," *The Huffington Post*, August 9, 2013.

A good negotiator is an active listener. While the appropriate and well-chosen arguments are necessary to be persuasive, persuasion should not only be about talking, monopolizing conversation, or taking pleasure listening to oneself. A person will be more receptive to your ideas if you give them a chance to talk. Listening attentively to people increases your chances of being trusted.[199] Combined with smiling and nodding, it creates positive feelings and encourages the person you are listening to talk in confidence.

To properly engage with your counterpart, you can adopt the tools of mirroring and matching. Essentially, you will subtly emulate their body language, tone of voice, breathing rhythms, emotional demeanor such as excitement or relaxation, phraseology, interests, even clothes to a certain extent. This can be a first step and it requires studying the subject and adopting what should be felt as closeness, not mimicry.

Have you had the surprising realization that you've unconsciously adopted the accent or intonations of the person you are chatting with sometimes? It happens to me with the French Swiss accent. An important community of Swiss bankers is part of my social and professional circle, and I find myself comfortably falling into the rhythms of their speech patterns occasionally. This type of unconscious mimicking facilitates human interactions by triggering liking and empathy.

An effective way to mirror a person and make them feel a connection is forming between you is to repeat words used by that person, so they feel that you are aligned with what they are saying. It is proven that a waitress repeating verbatim the order of patrons will increase the frequency of tipping and the amount of money she will make.[200] Retail salespeople using similar technique will have the same positive effect on customers.[201]

---

[199] Daniel R. Ames, Lily Benjamin Maissen, and Joel Brockner. "The role of listening in interpersonal influence." *Journal of Research in Personality* 46(3); (2012): 345-349.

[200] Céline Jacob and Nicolas Guéguen. "The effect of employees' verbal mimicry on tipping." *International Journal of Hospitality Management* 35 (2013): 109-111.

[201] Céline Jacob, Nicolas Guéguen, Angélique Martin, and Gaelle Boulbry. "Retail salespeople's mimicry of customers: Effects on consumer behavior." *Journal of Retailing and Consumer Services* 18 (2011): 381–388.

Another way of building rapport with others is placing yourself for a moment in the shoes of the person with whom you are trying to establish it. You may begin to experience what that person feels like under certain conditions. *Are they the only woman in the room? Do they speak the language in which the negotiations are being conducted? Are they comfortable and relaxed?* And so on. Noticing these things requires you to be observant and gives you the opportunity to be thoughtful. You would be surprised how simple gestures such as providing a box of tissues and pouring a glass of water for their seat at the table increases your likability and can lower tension in a room.

Being naturally curious and knowing a little bit about a lot of topics will keep you in a good stead. Getting familiar with many topics will give you a far better chance to engage in a conversation about an interest your counterpart holds dear. I am not a fan of Formula 1 as some people can be, but I know who the top champions are and who won the last race. I don't trade on the stock market, but I know the performance of the S&P 500, the price of gold and a barrel of oil. This knowledge allows me to participate in conversations and find out more easily what makes people tick. Negotiators should be readers and inform themselves constantly.

Human beings experience stress and discomfort when holding two opposite thoughts in their mind at the same time and these thoughts are unable to be reconciled. This is what scientists call "cognitive dissonance." It often triggers when a person is forced to make a choice between two relatively equal options or to justify their attitude. Your role as a negotiator is to reduce such stressful situations by making a choice obvious and the person feel good about it.

With rapport, a focus and positive affect are shared to create harmony.[202] Such harmony should be fostered, and tension defused in a subtle and appropriate way (e.g., a small gift or attention, a valuable introduction, or an invitation for dinner). The efforts one puts in small things helps you gain greater things further down the road.

---

[202] Linda Tickle-Degnen and Robert Rosenthal. "The Nature of Rapport and Its Nonverbal Correlates." *Psychological Inquiry* 1(4); (1990): 285-293.

No need to make your interest in the person too obvious, see an invitation turned down too easily, or worse, sound desperate. Avoid flattery, which can be seen as shallow or false, and practice genuine appreciation. Since negotiation is intended to yield something you really want, it is worth your time and effort to invest in a more nuanced and sincere approach.

You would be surprised how often one simple practice is overlooked. For instance, people don't take time to remember people's names. Yet, we all like to be called by our name. It feels like a compliment. People feel a special difference between "Good morning" and "Good morning, John." Dale Carnegie used to say *"Forget a name or misspell it – and you have placed yourself at a sharp disadvantage."*[203] You will get better attention from people when you call them by their names.

Note that we remember names better when we are fully present at the time of introduction and when we establish a true interest in the people we are introduced to. This is something you can practice every time you meet a new person. A good way to remember someone's name is to repeat it loud after being disclosed.

While David Brooks humorously describes rapport earlier as "an invasion of personal space," research concurs that quick and non-obtrusive touching can also increase trust for the touched person.[204] Jacob Hornik, professor in marketing and communications, conducted a 1991 experiment where *"286 shoppers were greeted by one of 6 student-experimenters while entering a bookstore. Half the shoppers were touched, and the other half were not. A light touch on the upper arm increased the subjects' shopping time, their amount of shopping, as well as their over-all evaluation of the store."*[205]

---

[203] Dale Carnegie, *How to Win Friends and Influence People* (New Delhi: Diamond Pocket Books, 2016), Kindle, Loc. 1179.

[204] Michael W. Kraus, Cassy Huang, and Dacher Keltner. "Tactile Communication, Cooperation, and Performance: An Ethological Study of the NBA." *Emotion,* Vol. 10(5); (2010): 745–749.

[205] Jacob Hornik. "Store Tactile Stimulation and Consumer Response," *Journal of Consumer Research* (1992), vol. 9, 449-457. *Perceptual and Motor Skills,* 73(3, Pt 1); (1991): 969-970.

However, be mindful of ways and areas that people don't like to be touched, especially as a difference must be made between men and women. A 2015 study investigated which part of their body people from Finland, France, Italy, Russia, and the United Kingdom allowed to be touched. The results depended on who touched them. They accepted to be touched more by acquaintances and family members.[206] Hands, arms, and eventually shoulders would be the best way to go with friends, acquaintances, and eventually strangers. To avoid awkward situations for negotiators, touch must be a quick gesture and not prolonged. Bear in mind that physical contact with people of a different gender is not well accepted in some cultures, and it is your responsibility as a negotiator to understand and act accordingly. I personally prefer to slightly and quickly touch the elbow of a person, especially when shaking hands or walking a person to a door. The reason is that, being a man or woman, people typically don't find the elbow too intrusive as a body part in most cultures, while the gesture simultaneously creates warmth and closeness.

You may also obtain more goodwill and cooperativeness from someone if you can trigger a positive affect in them as well. Positive affect is a behavior triggered by positive emotions or feelings such as enthusiasm, joy, pride, confidence, and so on. Positive emotions make people happy, relaxed, and more cooperative.

How do you trigger such positive affect? Smile, use appropriate humor, try to identify the favorite topic of a person, and avoid controversial topics. Common favorites are children or grandchildren, sports, travels, wine, and reading. Find an appropriate setting where the person will feel most comfortable, such as a restaurant where you can create and share a positive memorable experience and enhance their senses. Your time, when building rapport, should be at a minimum invested in the genuine understanding of your counterpart's motivations and interests. As Madeleine Albright once nicely put it, *"You don't have to like everybody, but you have to learn what*

---

[206] Julia T. Suvilehto, Enrico Glerean, Robin I. M. Dunbar, Riitta Hari, and Lauri Nummenmaa, "Topography of social touching depends on emotional bonds between humans," *PNAS*, 2015, Nov. 10; 112(45): 13811-13816.

makes them tick."[207]

Activating senses by providing something people can see, hear, and smell can be a powerful influential tool. This sensory engagement, if well played, can trigger positive emotions and stimulate curiosity. That way your ideas will stick on their mind better. You may have noticed that you remember better a movie when such movie has triggered emotions in you. The same principles apply to people you share time with.[208,209] This is one of the reasons I have chosen to support my business activities with memorable experiences in fine wines and gastronomy.

If a smile is good to build rapport, a genuine laugh is even better. However, not everyone has a natural comedic talent. Timing is essential and the type of humor must be well appreciated. Some people think that being funny means cracking jokes. In reality, most laughter is not triggered by jokes but by social interaction. According to neuroscientist Robert Provine:

> *banal comments like, "Where have you been?" or "It was nice meeting you, too" – hardly knee-slappers – are far more likely to precede laughter than jokes. Only 10% to 20% of the laughter episodes we witnessed followed anything joke-like. Even the most humorous of the 1,200 comments that preceded laughter weren't necessarily howlers: "You don't have to drink, just buy us drinks!" and "Was that before or after I took my clothes off?" being two of my favorites. This suggests that the critical stimulus for laughter is another person, not a joke.*[210]

---

[207] Robert O'Neill, "Albright, on negotiating," *The Harvard Gazette*, April 3, 2015.

[208] Lindsay Dodgson. "Getting emotional might actually help us remember things, not make us forget them." Business Insider, Jan. 5, 2017.

[209] Arielle Tambini, Ulrike Rimmele, Elizabeth Phelps, and Lila Davachi. "Emotional brain states carry over and enhance future memory formation." *Nature Neuroscience* 20(2); (2016): 271-278.

[210] Robert Provine. "The Science of Laughter: Far from mere reactions to jokes, hoots and hollers are serious business: They're innate – and important – social tools." *Psychology Today, November 1, 2000 – last reviewed on June 9, 2016.*

Relationships last longer when those relationships contain smiles and laughs. We don't choose friends who are funny, we choose friends with whom we can share laughter.

[25] The Road to Persuasion

> The highest achievers spent more time crafting what they did and said before making a request. They set about their mission as skilled gardeners who know that even the finest seeds will not take root in stony soil or bear fullest fruit in poorly prepared ground. They spent much of their time toiling in the fields of influence thinking about and engaging in cultivation—in ensuring that the situations they were facing had been pretreated and readied for growth. Of course, the best performers also considered and cared about what, specifically, they would be offering in those situations. But much more than their less effective colleagues, they didn't rely on the legitimate merits of an offer to get it accepted; they recognized that the psychological frame in which an appeal is first placed can carry equal or even greater weight.
>
> —Robert Cialdini[211]

Persuading is convincing someone to do something by giving them good reasons for it. Few can truly improvise persuasion, and the best persuaders are often people who have mastered the art of psychological framing. They come from a distance and prepare for the final blow.

It may be obvious for some, but to be persuasive it is critical that you first know what you are talking about. Some people can be surprisingly convincing without knowing what they are talking about, until sooner rather than later, they are confronted about their credibility and their reputation is undermined.

You should know more than enough about what you are selling and avoid venturing into unknown territories. Imagine a situation of a salesperson hot selling a new technology with limited knowledge of its functions

---

[211] Robert Cialdini, *Pre-Suasion: A Revolutionary Way to Influence and Persuade* (New York: Simon & Schuster, 2016), 4.

and properties. Would you easily trust this person? Probably not. As we already mentioned in Chapter 2 of this book, anticipation and intelligence are key factors of success in negotiation. You would not go fishing without your fishing poles. Unfortunately, some people think that the superiority of their intellect or their charming nature can compensate a lack of knowledge. Others think that their expertise in a field can save them. Daniel J. Boorstin, American historian, once said, *"The greatest enemy of knowledge is not ignorance, it is the illusion of knowledge."*[212] Seduce, but don't pitch what you don't clearly understand.

Knowledge will give you confidence and credibility as long as your ideas are clear and well organized. With exposure to too much information and too many decisions to be made at once, minds can easily get muddled. Don't lose yourself to a runaway train of thoughts and give the impression of confusion.

Keeping in mind the ancestral principles of rhetoric, as developed in the Ancient World, can be useful. The word "rhetoric" comes from the Greek *rhêtorikê tekhnê*, which translates to the *art of speaking*. The 5 canons of rhetoric appeared in Cicero's first-century Latin text, *Rhetorica ad Herennium*. They are a prime example of how to structure the mindset of a persuader to seduce, demonstrate, and move others. Your ideas (invention) should be:

- logically organized in your mind (arrangement)
- well memorized (memory)
- presented in the most appropriate fashion (style)
- efficiently offered to your audience (delivery)

Rhetoric certainly requires preparation and practice, but if the principles of this book, such as mindfulness, focus, insightful reading, and self-awareness, to name just a few, are followed, foggy brains should become clearer and thoughts more accurate. Persuasion is an art, but also a way of life.

Your mind must be able to quickly shift from prepared to agile. Supportive ideas should come out easily, and your style should be able to adjust from

---

[212] Carol Krucoff, "The 6 O'Clock Scholar," *The Washington Post*, January 29, 1984.

formal to casual or serious to humorous as need be. You should certainly switch off the negotiation button for the right occasions, but you must be able to switch it on again quickly because opportunities to negotiate are everywhere all the time. An agile mind is simple (in the sense that it aims at simplifying complex ideas), focused, curious, and detached (ability to put things in perspective).

Your message should be clear and not overly complex. If you confuse others, they may make irrational decisions out of frustration or boredom. The choice of your words is paramount. As Robert Greene, American author, said, *"the human tongue is a beast that few can master. It strains constantly to break out of its cage, and if it is not tamed, it will turn wild and cause you grief."*[213]

Although words only form a small part of the human communication palette, they are powerful. We speak, listen, and read every day even in the visual world we live in. Words can send signals of power, dominance, frustration, contempt, friendliness, and so much more. They can also trigger negative and positive emotions in others. A single word can mean the difference between liking and disliking, judgmental and nonjudgmental. Think, for instance, about the difference of impact on a person between "This is stupid" and "This is risky." One is judgmental and the other is an informed observation.

The more acceptable the words you use are, the more opportunities you will have to express your thoughts in a precise way. That's why reading is so important for a negotiator. The French dictionary Le Grand Robert currently contains 100,000 words and the Oxford dictionary contains 600,000 words. However, humans have an active and passive dictionary with known words they hardly or never use. This repertoire could help them to make themselves better understood or soften the edges for a better rapport, but they limit its use to a few thousand words, if not hundreds for some. Worse, many words are chosen unconsciously and attach to the emotions they feel at the time they say them.

---

[213] Robert Greene, *The 48 Laws of Power* (London: Profile Books Ltd, 2000), 33.

You may have noticed, for instance, that when we are frustrated, we often employ the same words. It could be, for instance, "terrible," "sick," "lame," "nuts," "shoot," or "loony." These same words can instantly come out of your mouth when you experience that frustration, like the lyrics of a favorite song you have listened over and over and which will come to your lips naturally. The high level of negativity they carry can have an adverse impact on the people hearing them, but also on yourself. Because they are associated with an emotion, they end up triggering that emotion when you employ them, and vice versa, sometimes with great intensity. There are no better words to describe this phenomenon than those of George Orwell: *"if thought corrupts language, language can also corrupt thought."*[214]

Seeing or hearing negative words triggers a neural change in our brain in the form of a production of stress hormones. People tend to raise their defenses when confronted with negative words. On the other hand, positive words are beneficial to both speaker and listener. Rather than stress hormones, positive words generate oxytocin, which acts as a neurotransmitter in the brain.[215] It is often referred to as the "love hormone" and increases bonding, trust, affinity, and empathy.

We do not realize that our language carries a lot of negativity and aggression. Some words and expressions have become so common that their origin, sometimes military, is largely forgotten (e.g., bullet points, targets, on standby, deadline, etc.).

Changing your vocabulary and softening your language as a negotiator can be greatly beneficial. It starts with self-awareness and the ability to properly identify the negative words used in connection with your most frequent negative emotions. The idea is then to replace them with softer ones to avoid any adverse psychological impact on yourself and others. It does not mean you can never say "no" or never use negative words, but you seek a more

---

[214] George Orwell, "Politics and the English Language," *Horizon Journal*, April 1946 (volume 13, issue 76), 262.

[215] Andrew Newberg, M.D., and Mark Robert Waldman, *Words Can Change Your Brain* (New York: Penguin Group, 2012), 23.

positive and constructive way to express your disagreement or negative emotions. Avoid harsh words and use the sandwich method for criticism: critics coming together with genuine appreciation and positive words. Expressing frank and direct criticism can be destructive and tarnish your reputation. Dale Carnegie used to compare criticisms to homing pigeons, and the fact they always return home.[216]

When it comes to positive words, "love" and "peace" are obviously more difficult to place in a business context but "yes," "great," "agree," "absolutely," and so on should be used more often.

Churchill was well known to spend a significant number of hours on the preparation of his speeches in search for the most accurate and powerful words. This is why they are still considered today as best examples of wisdom and eloquence. Churchill wrote his own speeches until the end of his life. He would draft them, sometimes through the help of his secretary, in the format of a poem to remember better where to pause and place emphasis. He would make numerous changes until the last minute and would learn them by heart. The following metaphor from 1943 would have been attributed to Churchill: *"A speech should be like a lady's dress –colorful enough to catch the attention, long enough to cover the subject and short enough to be interesting."*

Associating an image, analogy, or metaphor with your words adds power to them. People tend to remember better content delivered with images. Again, Churchill was skilled at using imagery to give strength to his words. In 1942, he met with Joseph Stalin in Moscow. Stalin was blaming the allies for not doing enough to defeat the Germans and wanted a landing in France to release pressure on the Eastern front. Winston Churchill flew to Moscow to try to persuade Stalin to organize an attack in North Africa instead. Churchill is remembered for having drawn a crocodile representing the Nazi Regime. The attack in North Africa was like attacking the most vulnerable part of a crocodile, its belly, according to Churchill.

---

[216] Dale Carnegie, *How to Win Friends and Influence People* (New York: Simon & Schuster, 1936, 1998), 8.

Metaphors provide more vivid descriptions of what we want to say.[217] Good metaphors help listeners to better understand the nuances and substance of our ideas. They activate analogies, trigger emotions, and resonate better in the listener's mind. These figures of speech have more impact at the beginning of a sentence or an argument than at the end, and the best metaphors are visual and not linguistic.

Metaphors can also reveal a lot about the personality or state of mind of the person telling them. For instance, the use of war metaphors in negotiation may reveal a propensity for an adversarial approach. Unfortunately, some negotiators are not always able to decode the metaphors of others because they are focusing more on what they themselves will say next.

It is better to send a concrete message to people we try to convince than an abstract one. Concreteness is about factual situations and specific examples. Concrete ideas make you sound clearer and more persuasive.

In the realm of persuasion, you must also be certain and convinced of your position when delivering your message. That's when a passion for or a dedication to the subject matter of the conversation can help. To convince efficiently, you should first believe what you are saying. If you doubt yourself of your message in important moments, you may appear weak and less credible. In your communication show no hesitance and always promote a clear vision with conviction. Honoré de Balzac, French novelist, once said that *"Conviction is human will attaining to its highest reach. At once, both cause and effect, it impresses the coldest natures; it is a species of mute eloquence which holds the masses."*[218]

Donald Trump is quite impressive in terms of conviction. When running for presidential election, he kept repeating over and over with certainty that a wall would be the solution to solve the Mexican immigration problem. Experts showed that in an interconnected world, a wall would not be efficient,

---

[217] Chip Heath and Dan Heath, *Made to Stick* (New York: Random House International Edition, 2010), 57.

[218] Honoré de Balzac, *The Works of Honoré de Balzac* (Boston: Roberts Brothers, 1890), 124.

that it would cost a fortune to build and maintain, and that division and stigmatization is not the solution to the immigration issue, and so on. Despite all these arguments, Trump managed to convince a large part of his electorate that it was the right thing to do, because he talked with absolute certainty. But being convinced doesn't mean you should not keep an open mind.

In communication there is a time when people are most receptive to your words, yet we tend to forget timing when it comes to influencing people. We often fail to project ourselves and anticipate other people's needs or mind frame.

If you manage to get a person to be present and to focus on something of importance to you, the message you are trying to share will be better received, and you will increase your chances of obtaining something positive out of the conversation. You need to ensure that at the time of persuasion you have the listener's maximum attention. The opportunity to negotiate at a time they are calm, undistracted, and relaxed should be your goal and for sure your endeavor if these conditions are not satisfied yet. The human attention span is narrow. It would now be just eight seconds (less than that of a goldfish).[219] The younger people are, the less attentive they are.

Lack of attention is often betrayed by the eyes. We move our eyes every 2 to 3 seconds on average, building what scientists call a priority map, which guides attention to the brain.[220] If the eyes of the person you are talking to are darting around excessively, you probably don't have their full attention. There could be many reasons for it. For instance, we are easily distracted by human faces. If you want to secure someone's attention, don't choose a place with too many people around. We also tend to focus our attention more readily to what we experienced positively in the past, as our brain orients our attention to what we like – a cake, for example. It then triggers memories and attention can easily be lost.

---

[219] Microsoft attention spans, Spring 2015.

[220] Eileen Kowler, "Eye movements: The past 25 years," *Vision Research* (2011), 51 (3), 1457-1483.

Our brains also love to drive our attention to new information. If you have an important meeting at the lounge of a hotel, and you are sitting at a table with magazines on it, your brain will encourage you to check the covers of the magazines or even the inside if the cover looks appealing. This also occurs with mobile phones and new messages popping up. As a negotiator in a situation of persuasion, try to avoid such unwanted distractions. Too much information coming at the same time to someone means more data and priorities to process for their brain. A brain focuses well on one thing or task at a time.

Limiting distractions doesn't mean that you should prefer simple settings for your negotiations over nice ones. There is an important difference between offering a pleasant atmosphere and an array of intriguing things to look at. Note that you will receive less attention if your counterparts are tired or stressed. Attend to their comfort as much as you can by providing comfortable seating and beverages like coffee and tea.

When I don't have people's attention at a meeting, I tend to remain silent. This happens sometimes when a person partially listens to you but also types emails or messages at the same time on their mobile phone or computer. They usually end up apologizing and expedite their task under silent pressure. If a person is too busy to listen to you, it is probably not the right time for a discussion. Better to let them finish what they are doing and come back to you with full attention.

I always try my best to schedule important negotiation meetings in the morning (9:00 a.m.-10:00 a.m.) or after lunch (2:00 p.m.-2:30 p.m.), when people are likely to have food in their stomach and have not processed a barrage of information yet.

In 2011, researchers from Ben Gurion University (Israel) and Columbia University, New York, published an interesting study. Their objective was to answer the following question: *Are judicial rulings based solely on laws and facts?* They analyzed 1,112 judicial rulings from 8 Jewish-Israeli judges over a period of 10 months. Prisoners consisted of 727 Jewish-Israeli males (65.3%), 326 Arab-Israeli males (29.3%), 50 Jewish-Israeli females (4.5%), and 9 Arab-Israeli females (0.9%). They looked into the judges' daily food breaks and found that *"when judges made repeated rulings, they showed an increased tendency to rule in favor of the status quo. This tendency was overcome by taking a break to eat a meal demonstrating the effects of glucose on mental resource replenishment."* The percentage of favorable rulings ended up reaching 65 percent after a break.[221]

Voltaire also noticed the importance of a full stomach for thinkers. In 1770, he wrote to his friend D'Alembert a letter in which he commented that *"thought depends absolutely on the stomach, but in spite of that, those who have the best stomachs are not the best thinkers."*[222] There is no reasoning with a starving man. That man is likely to direct his thoughts toward food or his watch rather than to what you are talking about.

The same principle of good timing applies to electronic communications. I also avoid sending important emails on a Friday, because many people are already on weekends in their heads and may give less importance to it. I find the best time slots for a recipient to receive important emails and messages to be between 10:00 a.m. and 11:00 a.m. and 2:00 p.m. to 3:00 p.m. from Monday to Thursday. But electronic communications add another layer of difficulty to negotiators. You must compete with other people's emails and messages and get attention. To have the odds on your side, you should pay particular attention to the subject of your correspondence (it should be catchy enough to gain attention) and the brevity of the content. It is also possible to double up email and instant messages when crucial.

---

[221] Shai Danziger, Jonathan Levav, and Liora Avnaim-Pesso. "Extraneous factors in judicial decisions." *Proceedings of the National Academy of Sciences*, 108 (17); (2011): 6889-6892.

[222] Voltaire, *Letter to d'Alembert, 20 August 1770,* Oeuvres Compete de Voltaire, Correspondances avec D'Alembert, Tome 2 (Paris: Chez Thomine et Fortic, Librairies, 1822), 164.

⌈IN ESSENCE⌋

- Influencing others does not consist of winning a debate of ideas or proving the superiority of an intellect but rather subtly making people like you to finally trust you so you can impact their decisions with your ideas.
- Build rapport before persuading. Rapport is a precondition to trust.
- Your time, when building rapport, should be at the minimum invested in the genuine understanding of your counterpart's motivations and interests.
- Be curious and familiar with many topics to stand a far better chance to engage in a conversation about interests of people you aim to influence.
- A person will be more receptive to your ideas if you give them a chance to talk.
- You will obtain more goodwill and cooperativeness from someone if you can trigger a positive affect in them.
- To be persuasive, first know what you are talking about.
- *The greatest enemy of knowledge is not ignorance, it is the illusion of knowledge.*
- Train your mind to be agile. Don't lose yourself to a runaway train of thoughts and miss the opportunity to persuade.
- In the realm of persuasion, you must be certain and convinced of your position, when delivering your message. Certainty and conviction should not be stubbornness.
- *The human tongue is a beast that few can master. It strains constantly to break out of its cage, and if it is not tamed, it will turn wild and cause you grief.*
- Associating an image, analogy, or metaphor with your words adds power to them.

- A single word can mean the difference between liking and disliking, judging and not judging. Pay attention to the power of your words.
- Your message is best delivered once the perfect scene has been arranged and your audience has been placed in a state of mind which makes them receptive to your ideas.

CHAPTER SIX:

Reach Your Peak

You cannot climb the ladder of success dressed in the costume of failure.

—Zig Ziglar[223]

You will achieve better outcomes as a negotiator if you are in peak condition. We now have a better understanding of the human brain, body, and social behaviors. We can go deep in understanding ourselves and others and turn that understanding into an advantage.

As basic as it sounds, living a balanced life, staying in good shape, and sharpening your mind help you stay ahead of the game in the long run. Negotiators should prefer excellence to excess. After all, negotiation is a question of compromise and not extremes. *"Whoever loves horses and dogs too much, displeases women; and he who loves women too much, displeases God. Therefore, govern your tastes, and brindle your inclinations."*[224] These were the wise words of Victor Hugo in 1842, and they still echo today.

The image that a negotiator reflects is also key to their success, as the impression we give is intrinsically linked to trust. While remaining authentic, consistently sending positive messages to the outside world contributes to generate a good opinion.

---

[223] https://www.ziglar.com/.

[224] Victor Hugo, *The Rhine* (London: D. Aird, 1843) Letter XXI: 172.

⌈26⌋ Develop a Personal Brand

> If you have a powerful personal brand, you lead more, you win more, and you earn more.
>
> —Ann Bastianelli[225]

Your personal brand is what you present and how you are perceived by others. It includes your reputation, style, and behaviors you are known or remembered for.

Ultimately, your brand shapes the opinion people form about you. Therefore, it is in your best interest to not only have a brand, but to strive to build a good one. With a powerful personal brand, people can be attracted to you like ants to honey. Humans constantly compare themselves to others, often seeking guidance and inspiration.

No one is entitled to the positive opinions of others. You must earn them. Consistently delivering signals leaves a memorable impression in the minds of people who encounter you. If these signals are positive, then you have a better chance to leave a positive impression, but if they are negative, you will have to work harder to gain the trust of others. For instance, a display of honesty, empathy, humbleness, a valuable network, or some notable achievements may instill trust in others. Even wearing the right clothes and representing well the products and services you are selling may help to achieve the objective of establishing a credible personal brand.

Your personal brand requires you to tap in your values and strengths and capitalize on them. These attributes need to be expressed in a genuine and authentic story. Your method should not be bragging on social media, but building a compelling and constant core that engages people to the point that

---

[225] "Powerful Personal Branding | Ann Bastianelli | TEDxWabashCollege" YouTube Video, 22:22, "TEDx Talks" February 22, 2017. https://www.youtube.com/watch?v=hcr3MshYe3g/.

they end up telling others about you. Your personal brand should follow you everywhere and precede you in any negotiation meetings you may attend. People you are dealing with should not only expect a pitch from you but also look forward to meeting you, enjoy your presence, and to the highest extent possible be inspired by you.

The master of constructing a meaningful personal brand is Sir Richard Branson. Branson has always considered that people relate to companies that have a face. His personal brand now even eclipses the Virgin brand. Branson has built a public profile that serves his businesses. He memorably dressed like a stewardess to promote Virgin Atlantic and crossed the Atlantic in a hot air balloon. People relate to his fun and friendly personal brand. The same people trust his ventures and buy his products as they see, consciously or unconsciously, a reflection of his personality in them.

Branson understood that it would be difficult to challenge Coca-Cola and British Airways through traditional marketing. His strategy was to use his own image on the front pages and make a fool of himself to build notoriety, but then always deliver indispensable quality and reliability.

CEOs like Branson depend less on traditional media now to share their biographies, stories, and vision. A digital world allows them to communicate directly to customers, stakeholders, or even voters for some of them. In the US, more than a third of the market value of corporations is attributed to their CEOs.[226]

The culture of image characterizes our times. Similar to the time when some of us quickly embraced emails as a new form of communication, those who accept that the world has changed and now requires us to stand out in a noisy crowd will have the odds on their side.

I know a few businesspeople and negotiators who are reluctant to disclose too much about themselves or their opinions. While their reserve could be understandable, it does not consider the change of context surrounding them. Their cautious approach might lead to isolation or disadvantages

---

[226] Weber Shandwick Inc. "The CEO Reputation Premium: Gaining Advantage in the Engagement Era." 2015.

that less reserved personalities may not endure. As we speak, 70 percent of employers use social media to screen candidates, and this number will continue increasing.[227] Recruiting and profiling algorithms are being developed and constantly upgraded. With the gig economy, organizations are offered the great opportunity to engage independent workers on a short-term basis and avoid hiring costly full-time employees. Within ten years, freelance workers may represent more than 50 percent of the US working population.[228] Freelancers need an online presence and therefore a personal brand. The way they appear and communicate is key to their success. Disclosure of personal information can create vulnerability, but it can also help build trust and gain credibility. In order to avoid unintended side effects, public disclosure should be thoughtful, honest, consistent, timely managed and to the most positive extent possible. It is true that a negotiator should remain minimally discreet and not show all their cards, but discretion regarding your intentions, your plans, and your strategy is in service of, not in conflict with, your personal brand. *"A continual reserve is like the lock on a door which is never turned and becomes so rusty that in the end no man can open it."*[229] There were the wise words of François de Callières in 1716.

Your image is your responsibility, and if you don't take control of it in a digital world, other people may do it for you. Unless you have lived a completely disconnected life, some information has already seeped into the Internet, such as tags, a photo, a phone number, an article, your profile on your company's website or on social media, and so on.

The ubiquity of the Internet doesn't mean that you should fall into the extreme of becoming a social media addict. Rather, it means that your image should be properly managed and your message out to the world aligned with

---

[227] CareerBuilder, "More Than Half of Employers Have Found Content on Social Media That Caused Them NOT to Hire a Candidate, According to Recent CareerBuilder Survey." 2018.

[228] Morgan Stanley Inc., "The Gig Economy Goes Global." 2018.

[229] Francois de Callières, *On the Manner of Negotiating with Princes* (New York: Houghton Mifflin, 2000), 20.

who you are, your values, and your actions. You are not enhancing your ego or necessarily becoming a celebrity. You are not making yourself a spam magnet or a troll target either. You are making yourself present and credible.

Remember that we are all judged by what we show. *Can people trust us? Can people respect us?* You should always look accessible, competent, and trustworthy at the time of doing business. People don't realize the opportunity they have to control their image and build their personal brand nowadays. In the old days, a personal image was often the result of testimonies and rumors. Only a limited number of people could afford to build their personal brand using traditional media.

Your reputation is inherent to your personal brand and the image it carries. Both can quickly be compromised if your actions lead to a loss or damages to the people or corporations you negotiate with or for. In 2018, 8 top executives of Lafarge, a world-leading French company producing cement, concrete, and aggregates, were accused in France of having paid 13 million Euros to terrorists to keep a factory open in war-torn Syria.

Even if these executives are proven to be innocent at the end, the damage to their reputation and that of their employer is significant and costly. They are now all tagged for who knows how long. This is an extreme case, but it provides an example of how serious the consequences may be when the borders of legality and ethics are tested (if not crossed). It takes years to build a good reputation in business, but it can take only a minute to destroy it.

If you come to the negotiation table with the reputation of being unfair, dishonest, a gossip, or an unethical negotiator, your counterpart will rightly be on the defensive (if they accept to deal with you in the first place). They will be cautious, and less inclined to make concessions. A good reputation brings more business and better business referrals. I personally prefer doing business and negotiating with people who have earned a successful reputation for generating money for themselves but also for their partners. These are win-win partners.

If a good reputation should be the soil in which your personal brand is rooted, your style should be the flower. *"Style is personal. It has nothing to do with fashion. Fashion is over quickly. Style is forever"* is a perfect sentiment, commonly attributed to Ralph Lauren.

In most instances, your appearance is the first information people process about you.[230] Image conveyed by clothing impacts human perceptions of others' financial success, authority, trustworthiness, intelligence, suitability for hire or promotion, and more.[231] First impressions made with your style can be very persistent (especially negative ones) and dominate people's thoughts regardless of how these impressions are challenged or contradicted.[232] If you are not conscientious of the impact, your style can become the enemy of your words, as it reveals social cues to others that may be at odds with your actions. What you wear triggers messages to the people around you. If this message does not align with your words or body language, there is incongruence, or "something feels off," as people say. You appear false. My advice is to always look clean and elegant as a negotiator.

Wear well-fitted and tasteful formal or smart casual. Try to find a balance between ordinary and daring. *"Pare down to the essence, but don't remove the poetry,"*[233] to use the words of Leonard Koren.

Experiment to find the right colors to meet the expectations. Colors can send hidden messages. As we know, human behavior is influenced by unconscious cues. Colors trigger associations in the minds of people. Red, for instance, is often perceived as dominant and aggressive, and people exposed

---

[230] Laura P. Naumann, Simine Vazire, Peter J. Rentfrow, and Samuel D. Gosling. "Personality Judgments Based on Physical Appearance." *Personality and Social Psychology Bulletin* 35(12); (2009):1661-71.

[231] Neil Howlett, Karen Pine, Ismail Orakcioglu, and Ben C. Fletcher. "The influence of clothing on first impressions: Rapid and positive responses to minor changes in male attire." *Journal of Fashion Marketing and Management* 17 (2013): 38-48.

[232] Bertram Gawronski, Robert J. Rydell, Bram Vervliet, and Jan De Houwer. "Generalization Versus Contextualization in Automatic Evaluation." *Journal of Experimental Psychology: General* 139(4); (2010): 683-701.

[233] Leonard Koren. *Wabi-Sabi for Artists, Designers, Poets & Philosophers* (Berkeley, CA: Stonebridge Press, 1994), 72.

to it tend to subconsciously conform to it.[234] You may be surprised to hear that tae kwon do, boxing, and wrestling athletes who wore red jerseys during the 2004 Olympic Games won more often than those wearing blue jerseys.[235] Donald Trump almost always wearing red ties may not be just a coincidence. Conversely, research shows for women wearing red often triggers sexual attraction from men.[236] Green is often seen as a balancer, whereas blue would convey calm and confidence.

Pay attention to your shoes; they needn't be brand-new and gleaming, but they must be clean and in good condition. It has been proven that others can accurately assess our personality based on the quality of our shoes. In a study conducted at the University of Kansas, researchers showed participants photos of other test subject's shoes and asked the observers to draw conclusions about the shoes owners' personalities, genders, and socioeconomic statuses. They *"concluded that attractiveness and comfort of shoes is a particularly interpretable reflection of the owner's personal characteristics."*[237]

As with so much in life, balance is important. Never overdress, and try, to the best extent possible, to not contrast too much with your counterpart. Remember that people tend to be friendlier with people who are alike. If you apply for a job in a start-up where everyone is casual and laid-back, too much formality in your attire may not be appropriate for the situation and unintentionally signal that you are not the right fit for the culture.

The key is the image you want to convey. If you are a doctor wearing a lab coat, you will look more credible and your authority will less likely be

---

[234] Diana Wiedemann, D. Michael Burt, Russell A. Hill, and Robert A. Barton. "Red clothing increases perceived dominance, aggression and anger," *Biology Letters*, The Royal Society Publishing, 11(5); (2015).

[235] Dennis Dreiskaemper, Bernd Strauss, Norbert Hagemann, and Dirk Büsch. "Influence of Red Jersey Color on Physical Parameters in Combat Sports." *Journal of Sport & Exercise Psychology* 35, (2013): 44-49.

[236] Adam D. Pazda, Andrew J. Elliot, and Tobias Greitemeyer, "Sexy red: Perceived sexual receptivity mediates the red-attraction relation in men viewing woman," *Journal of Experimental Social Psychology* 48(3); (2011):787–790.

[237] Omri Gillath, Angela Bahns, Fiona Ge, and Christian S. Crandall. "Shoes as a source of first impressions." *Journal of Research in Personality* 46(4); (2012): 423–430.

challenged than if you wear a casual top. The same is true with lawyers and suits. Suits and uniforms convey authority and respect, and possibly even conformism from others.

Don't show too much of your skin, and always press or iron your clothes. Mind your haircut and hairstyle. The same is true with shaving or barbering if you are a man, as an unkempt beard is not a sign of someone who necessarily attends to the details. These seemingly small details attest to your commitment to respect yourself and those who are investing their time with you. I saw people in Asia attending initial business meetings in shorts and flip-flops when they were far from being successful or powerful enough to get away with it. They start a discussion with a handicap without realizing it. They think they are smart enough to compensate for a poor first impression.

What we wear does not only have an impact on others, but it also influences the way we think about ourselves.[238] We unconsciously adopt the characteristics of what we wear. For instance, if we wear casual clothes, we tend to be more relaxed in our attitude. Some clothes can also make us feel more confident and powerful. An American study shows that formal clothing encourages abstract thinking and people think more broadly and holistically wearing it.[239]

Pleasant scents also positively affect the social atmosphere and put people in a positive mood. The positive impact of scent is why you find nice aromas in shopping malls, boutiques, and hotels.[240,241,242] Marketers are smart.

---

[238] Lydia Dishman, "The Surprising Productivity Secrets Hidden in Your Clothes," *Fast Company*, February 28, 2014.

[239] Michael L. Slepian, Simon N. Ferber, Joshua M. Gold, and Abraham M. Rutchick. "The Cognitive Consequences of Formal Clothing." *Social Psychological and Personality Science* 6(6); (2015): 661-668.

[240] Nicolas Guéguen. "Women Exposure to Pleasant Ambient Fragrance and Receptivity to a Man's Courtship Request." *Chemosensory Perception* (2011), 4(4).

[241] Robert A. Baron. "The Sweet Smell of… Helping: Effects of Pleasant Ambient Fragrance on Prosocial Behavior in Shopping Malls." *Personality and Social Psychology Bulletin* 23(5); (1997): 397-400.

[242] Nicolas Gueguen and Christine Petr. "Odors and consumer behavior in a restaurant," *International Journal of Hospitality Management* 25 (2006): 335–339.

They have long understood that scents can entice consumers and heighten value perception. Smell is linked to memory and triggers emotions. People can remember and distinguish smells with a fair level of accuracy.[243] Scientists posit that humans can detect more than a trillion odor mixtures[244] and predict with fair accuracy the personality traits of a person (such as anxious, social, or sympathetic) based on their body odor.[245] *"A woman's perfume tells more about her than her handwriting,"* Christian Dior is reputed to have said.

My advice here is simply this: do not underestimate your style when negotiating. If you are prepared to make that effort for a job interview or a date, you should also be prepared to make the same effort to attend strategic negotiations. Combined with communication skills, your style can be an unsuspected influential tool. Better to paint a positive image immediately in the minds of people rather make up lost opportunities.

[27] Set the Bar

A healthy body is a guest-chamber for the soul; a sick body is a prison.
—Francis Bacon[246]

Negotiation doesn't only require you to be expert in your field and be a good communicator, it also requires you to be alert, fit, and sharp. Negotiators should seek a performance lifestyle that does not let them go off the tracks. Balance is the essence.

---

[243] Bryan Walsh, "Your Nose Can Smell at Least 1 Trillion Scents," *Time*, March 20, 2014.

[244] The Rockefeller University, "Sniff study suggests humans can distinguish more than 1 trillion scents," March 20, 2014.

[245] Agnieszka Sorokowska. "Assessing Personality Using Body Odor: Differences Between Children and Adults." *Journal of Nonverbal Behavior* 37(3); (2013): 153–163.

[246] This quote is generally attributed to Francis Bacon.

As we mentioned earlier in this book, the life of a business negotiator can sometimes be hectic with long hours, little sleep, travels, work on laptops or smartphones in taxis or hotel lobbies, not forgetting a questionable diet. It can be easy to lose focus, be forgetful, or get a clouded mind when the time comes to negotiate. A life-business balance is key to perform well in the long term.

Developing positivity, meditating, resting, unplugging, and eating well are suggestions we have already made to increase negotiators' performance. But we should also underline the importance of routines in a world of growing complexity.

Aristotle considered that *"We are what we repeatedly do. Excellence then is not an act, but a habit."*[247] Daily routines and habits, even if simple and discrete, help us to stay on the right track and be more successful. It starts with a bit of self-awareness and some scrutiny in the way we spend our time every day. It follows with spotting opportunities to get better.

Some routines can be specific to negotiators, but some should be common to them. Finding time to read every day is a habit of high achievers. Catching the early worm is another. You are more likely to set good habits and be less reactive to your environment if you wake up early. Early risers tend to procrastinate less, have time to wake up properly and a better chance to eat a healthy breakfast, and exercise. They are less vulnerable to substance abuse and depression as well.[248] They have been proven to be overall more proactive and successful than night owls. The structure of the brain between larks and owls is actually different. Owls have less white matter, which facilitates communication among nerve cells.[249] A reduction of white matter in

---

[247] Will Durant, *The Story of Philosophy: The Lives and Opinions of the World's Greatest Philosophers*. Ch. II: Aristotle and Greek Science; part VII: Ethics and the Nature of Happiness (New York: Simon & Schuster, 1991), 87.

[248] Linda Geddes, "First physical evidence of why you're an owl or a lark," *New Scientist*, September 30, 2013.

[249] Jessica Rosenberg, Ivan I. Maximov, Martina Reske, Farida Grinberg, and N. Jon Shahab. "'Early to bed, early to rise': Diffusion tensor imaging identifies chronotype-specificity.' *NeuroImage* 84 (2014): 428-434.

the brain is linked to cognitive instability and a decrease in performance.[250]

In 2009, Christoph Randler, biologist and researcher at the University of Tübingen, published the results of a study. He asked 367 university students a set of questions about the time of the day they are more energized, their schedules, and sleep patterns. His conclusion was the following: *"When it comes to business success, morning people hold the important cards. My earlier research showed that they tend to get better grades in school, which get them into better colleges, which then lead to better job opportunities. Morning people also anticipate problems and try to minimize them, my survey showed. They're proactive. A number of studies have linked this trait, proactivity, with better job performance, greater career success, and higher wages."*[251]

Taking breaks during the day is another good habit to develop as it fosters productivity and creativity. Being able to maintain focus for a prolonged period of time is important for a negotiator. Short breaks such as brief walks or tea breaks (not so much social media breaks) significantly improve focus and reduce chances of losing vigilance on tasks.

A few minutes of exercise is highly beneficial as well, not only to your body but also to your brain. According to scholars from the Robinson Research Institute (University of Adelaide):

> *plasticity in the brain is important for learning, memory and motor skill coordination. The more "plastic" the brain becomes, the more it's able to reorganise itself, modifying the number and strength of connections between nerve cells and different brain areas. This exercise-related change in the brain may, in part, explain why physical activity has a positive effect on memory and higher-level functions.*[252]

---

[250] Anders M. Fjell, Lars. T. Westlye, Inge K. Amlien, and Kristine B. Walhovd. "Reduced White Matter Integrity Is Related to Cognitive Instability," *Journal of Neuroscience* 31(49); (2011): 18060-18072.

[251] Christoph Randler, "Defend Your Research: The Early Bird Really Does Get the Worm," *Harvard Business Review*, July-August 2010.

[252] The University of Adelaide, "Just 30 Minutes of Exercise Has Benefits for the Brain." October 2014.

Richard Branson believes he can be twice as productive in a single day by working out every day.[253] His regimen includes tennis, biking, and kitesurfing.[254] As the ex-president of the US, Barack Obama exercised about 45 minutes per day, 6 days a week.[255] He lifted one day and did cardio the next. Exercise is a great way to relieve stress. If you are always stressed, your brain will be submerged with stress hormones that can destroy your memory and damage your vital organs.[256] Knowing that exercise can help you discharge these stress hormones and clear your mind, why wouldn't you seek the benefits of physical activity?

Jack Dorsey, co-founder of Twitter, is a man of routine. *"I look to build a lot of consistent routine. Same thing every day. Allows a steady state that enables me to be more effective when I do have to react to something out of band,"* says Dorsey.[257] Like Tony Robbins,[258] Dorsey is a strong advocate of regular cold-water immersion, so he can cleanse his body, improve cardiovascular circulation, and enhance his mental performance.

The idea is of course not necessarily to suggest you immerse yourself in cold water every day to improve your performance as a negotiator, but to show you that successful businesspeople have come to efficient basic routines they stick to and adjust. They understand that it is easy to go off track without a road map and marking poles. Routines don't deserve the boring connotation people like to give them.

Like athletes, some of the best business leaders reach a steady continuous stream of performance through flow. In his book titled *The Rise of Superman:*

---

[253] "Richard Branson on Exercise and Productivity" YouTube Video, 0:51, "FourHourBodyPress" March 16, 2011. https://www.youtube.com/watch?v=QFjgMKwpz_k&feature=youtu.be/.

[254] Kathleen Elkins, "Richard Branson wakes up at 5 a.m. every morning—here's his daily routine," CNBC, April 11, 2017.

[255] The Editors of Men's Health, "Heroes of Health and Fitness," *Men's Health*, April 28, 2015.

[256] David Perlmutter, *The Better Brain Book: The Best Tool for Improving Memory and Sharpness and Preventing Aging of the Brain* (New York: Riverhead Books, 2004).

[257] Product Hunt, chat with Jack Dorsey, December 22, 2015.

[258] Team Tony, "The Power of (Cold) Water: 5 Surprising Health Benefits of Cold Water Immersion," *Tony Robbins Blog*.

Decoding The Science of Ultimate Human Performance, Steven Kotler describes "flow" as *"an optimal state of consciousness, a peak state where we both feel our best and perform our best. Action and awareness merge. Time flies. Self-vanishes. Performance goes through the roof."* During flow, the brain is altered and *"energy usually used to high cognitive functions is traded for heightened attention and awareness."*[259] More creativity is triggered. Attention becomes unbreakable and you become highly adaptable to situations.

According to James Olds, a neuroscientist and director of the Krasnow Institute mentioned by Kotler, *"you don't need giant waves or big mountains to trigger these responses [...] the brain's reaction isn't dependent on real, external information. It's reacting to a constellation of inputs from the sensory system. If you can light up the same constellation – let's say replace the novelty found in a natural environment with new routines in your daily life – you will get the dopamine and norepinephrine."*[260]

You don't have to be an athlete with extraordinary abilities to reach a state of effortless concentration and efficiency. We all regularly experience intense moments when we feel truly present and committed. Very often flow is linked to passion (something we really like to do) and performance (higher objectives than average). It is triggered by activity and not passivity. Flow happens when you have clarity in your goals, a commitment to achieve them, and you are able to receive immediate feedback as you progress. You know exactly what you have to do despite the challenge. You adjust and learn along the way.

Flow can be encouraged by limiting distractions, developing focus, setting up efficient routines, and so forth. Successful musicians, surgeons, writers, inventors, CEOs, and more have reached levels of excellence by entering the flow. The more you throw at that flow channel, the higher your chances are to perform well and feel good about it.

---

[259] Steven Kotler, *The Rise of Superman: Decoding the Science of Ultimate Human Performance* (New York: Houghton Mifflin, 2014), Preface and 49.

[260] Steven Kotler, *The Rise of Superman: Decoding the Science of Ultimate Human Performance* (New York: Houghton Mifflin, 2014), 105.

[28] Those Personal Traits

> An equable humour, a tranquil and patient nature, always ready to listen with attention to those whom he meets are things that are indispensable adjuncts to the negotiator's profession.
>
> —François de Callières[261]

Given the importance of negotiation in our lives and especially when doing business, the question we must ask is: What are the qualities that make some negotiators more effective than others beyond age, sex, status, education, motivations, and even intelligence?

We saw in Chapter One that the best negotiators all have a different style and that external factors have sometimes played an important role in their success. We have tackled a number of requisites for negotiators to be more successful, such as being emotionally intelligent, self-aware, focused, and positive. Are there any other basic character attributes negotiators should develop or that should be highlighted? The answer is yes, and these are some of the most important.

CALM

This should be a no-brainer. You have a better lasting influence on others if you stay calm and avoid raising defenses. Composure will always deliver better outcomes in negotiations and in the long run. You can be perfectly firm when necessary, but you should remain calm.

To achieve this objective, stress management, self-awareness, and efficient daily routines are keys. Breathing, exercise, sleep, limited coffee, meditation, and more should help to keep an inner calm. Some habits may be more

---

[261] François de Callières, *On the Manner of Negotiating with Princes* (New York: Houghton Mifflin, 2000), 19.

effective on you than others. It is your opportunity and responsibility to find it out.

Pressure is almost inevitable in modern societies, but mistakes triggered by anger are often avoidable. The trick is not so much to force yourself to be calm but embrace crisis to a point that the challenge becomes exciting. We all know that life sometimes does not go our way, that most successful people stumbled and failed before breaking through, and that our existence is far from a straight line to success. If we let things heat up every time we encounter a difficulty, we are promised a life of stress and deficiencies. One risk of being angry is revealing important or confidential information to others. Another risk is a negative impact on your reputation.

Emotions are contagious. You can transfer calmness to other people the same way you can transfer your positiveness. However, humans catch negative emotions more easily than positive ones as a result of our evolutionary past. Some people are also more sensitive than others to negative emotions for various reasons, and you often don't know it. Prudence should dictate calmness.

It is normal to experience anger or aggressiveness at some point. We all feel it coming up sometimes, but we should not remain in the path of anger. There is space between the stimulus and the response, and that's where you find your power to choose. *"The soul is composed of terrible poisons,"* said Honoré de Balzac, *"wanting burns us up and being able destroys us: but knowing leaves our weak organization in a perpetual of calm."*[262]

PATIENCE

We live in an impatient world of instant gratification. We are encouraged to think fast and move quick, making the art and virtue of patience sometimes more difficult to practice than ever. Yet, that only makes it more valuable to possess, and patience remains truly a key quality of a good negotiator.

Though occasionally business opportunities may be missed by being too cautious, rushing can also have disastrous consequences. This is the case if

---

[262] Harold Bloom, *Honoré de Balzac* (Philadephia: Chelsea House, 2003), 218.

you overlooked your obligations or the price you have accepted to pay is too high. For those who have seen the movie *Whiplash*, it may remind you of that scene when the music teacher Terence Fletcher slaps his student Andrew in the face when playing drums, demanding, *"Are you rushing or are you dragging?" "I don't know,"* answers Andrew. Fletcher counts off, *"One, two, three, four ... Rushing or dragging?"* Andrew, in tears, responds, *"Rushing."* Fletcher retorts, *"So you know the difference!"* It is a dramatic scene, but bear in mind that negotiation is a question of tempo. You have to know when to push things and when to slow them down to avoid painful disappointments.

It is certainly difficult to be patient sometimes, especially when the stakes are high, and we evolve in a highly competitive environment. Taking our time can also have a cost. However, the best deals we strike are generally those we are not desperate to close. Issues must be properly addressed and not brushed off or ignored for the sake of closing sooner rather than later. Yes, patience has limits, but patience pays off better than impulsivity. This is why philosophers, theologians, writers, and other thinkers have been praising its virtue for centuries.

Of course, some negotiations can be easy and straightforward but let's face it, the reality is that there is often a gap in term of demands or expectations between parties, and this gap needs to be bridged. High risk can make people think twice before they commit. Trust has to be gained first. Cultural differences can cause information to be lost in translation. Due diligence can reveal an unexpected liability. Lawyers can serve impediments to their negotiators with compliance and so on.

Patience means that we accept to delay things without getting upset or stressed about it. Delaying can be a question of minutes, hours, days, weeks, months, or even years. There are different kinds of patience: patience with difficult people, patience in front of challenging obstacles, and finally, the day-to-day difficulties we can encounter, from waiting for a late person to the printer not working that morning.

When Richard Branson heard that Necker Island (Virgin Islands) was for sale, he first offered $100,000 for it. The owner, Lord Cobham, refused it immediately, as his asking price was $6 million! Branson knew the price was too low but kept increasing it to avoid losing the relationship with Lord Cobham. Branson waited until Lord Cobham desperately needed the money. Branson finally bought it for $180,000 at the age of 28![263] Branson's patience paid off.

Warren Buffet is another legendarily patient leader. Each of his wise words are golden for most stock market investors around the world. He once compared investing in stocks to baseball and recommended patience to impulsive investors. Negotiators should find inspiration in these words coming from one of the most successful business investors of all time:

- **(Buffet):** *In the securities business, you sit there and they throw U.S. Steel at 25 and they throw General Motors at 16. You don't have to swing at any of them. They may be wonderful pitches to swing at but if you don't know enough, you don't have to swing. And you can sit there and watch thousands of pitches and finally get one right there where you wanted something that you understand and then you swing.*
- **(Goodman):** *So you might not swing for 6 months?*
- **(Buffet):** *Might not swing for two years.*
- **(Goodman):** *Isn't that boring?*
- **(Buffet):** *It will bore most people and certainly boredom is a problem with most professional money managers.*[264]

Dealing with impatience requires a dose of self-awareness. Triggers have to be identified and quickly addressed with anti-stress responses. Remember that there is always space between the stimulus and the response. It could be: "Is this important email I want to send tonight urgent? Can it wait until tomorrow to be sent, so I can sleep on it and go through it again with a fresh eye?"

---

[263] Richard Branson, "How I bought Necker Island," Virgin.com, August 25, 2015.

[264] "Warren Buffett's First Television Interview – Discussing Timeless Investment Principles" YouTube Video, 7:29, "Sanket Sigdel" November 30, 2017. https://www.youtube.com/watch?time_continue=2&v=T6HHwOoq9M4/.

Cultivating the virtue of patience is also being able to adjust your lifestyle. We sometimes try to do too much in one day and set the bar a bit too high. We end up running after time all day and stressing out. We can also waste precious time surfing without thinking on social media, whereas that time could be used for insightful reading, a respite, or useful meditation. Daily coffee intake can be reduced as well. We just need a bit of courage to look at our daily life and make some lasting changes. Effects may not be immediate, but I guarantee you it will help. You don't need to be born patient. You can become patient.

Patient people are proven to be more cooperative and more social than impatient ones.[265] Negotiation being a question of compromise and reciprocity, patient negotiators certainly have something extra up their sleeves. However, sound judgment should always suggest if time is being wasted either on a deal, a relationship, or an investment opportunity. Red flags should not be ignored. Being patient doesn't mean one should be blind and avoid cutting loose when circumstances present a threat.

CREATIVITY

To transcend initial rejection and overcome obstacles, a skilled negotiator must engage their creativity and generate ideas. Negotiation is a conflict of interests where gaps must be bridged, discrepancies ironed out, and accord reached. Creative negotiators can best generate solutions when they are not singularly focused on their own needs and instead looking at mutually beneficial outcomes.

The antithesis of a creative negotiator will be a person strictly abiding by the rules, going by the book, or sticking to a line of conduct no matter what. They see novelty as a threat to their objectives. They lack flexibility and have few alternatives to offer. They let fear drive their actions.

---

[265] Oliver S. Curry, Michael E. Price, and Jade G. Price, "Patience is a virtue: Cooperative people have lower discount rates," *Personality and Individual Differences,* 44 (2008) 778–783.

If your mind is trained to be creative you will be more resourceful and therefore you improve the quality of your deals.[266] Research has shown, for instance, that attending a creative workshop to prepare for an important negotiation helps negotiators to find integrative solutions that are mutually beneficial.[267]

There are certainly people born creative, such as Mozart and Leonardo da Vinci, although their success was probably the result of a number of circumstances. Yet, creativity can be learned and encouraged. Contrary to Nietzsche, I don't think *you need to have chaos in yourself to give birth to a dancing star.*[268] Ideas just need the right compost to grow. Patterns can be adopted to foster creativity.

In 2018, *Ophthalmology* published a study in which researchers enrolled a group of ophthalmology students for 3 months in art training class taught by professional art educators at the Philadelphia Museum of Art. Observation and descriptive skills of the students significantly improved after the class was over.[269] The ability to focus attention with full awareness is known to foster creativity.[270]

So, how do you become more creative as a negotiator?

Take time to think, disconnect, and read (not only books in your field). Reading books is highly beneficial and a great way to sharpen your mind.

---

[266] Elizabeth Ruth Wilson and Leigh L. Thompson, (2014),"Creativity and negotiation research: the integrative potential," *International Journal of Conflict Management*, Vol. 25 no. 4, 359-386.

[267] D. T. Ogilvie and Shalei Simms. "The Impact of Creativity Training on an Accounting Negotiation." *Group Decision and Negotiation* 18(1); (2009): 75-87.

[268] Friedrich Nietzsche, *Thus Spoke Zarathustra: A Book for All and None* (Cambridge: Cambridge University Press, 2006), First Part, 5, 9.

[269] Jaclyn Gurwin, Karen E. Revere, Suzannah Niepold, Barbara Bassett, Rebecca Mitchell, Stephanie Davidson, Horace DeLisser, and Gil Binenbaum. "A Randomized Controlled Study of Art Observation Training to Improve Medical Student Ophthalmology Skills." *Ophthalmology*, 125(1); (2018): 8-14.

[270] Matthijs Baas, Barbara Nevicka, and Femke S. Ten Velden. "Specific Mindfulness Skills Differentially Predict Creative Performance," *Personality and Social Psychology Bulletin*, Vol. 40(9); (2014): 1092–1106.

Reading stimulates the mind and increases emotional intelligence.[271] Books can also strengthen a vocabulary. Look into the lives of great business leaders, and you will likely find that most of them are avid readers, using reading to stay on top of new trends. Bill Gates reads around 50 books a year,[272] and Warren Buffet reads hundreds of pages a day (and not only financial reports).

Exchange ideas with others, including creative people. Visit and travel. Be curious and keep an open mind. Set some effective routines. Take care good care of your brain and body. Take notes. Ideas will follow. Just be consistent.

Negotiation is a problem-solving exercise. It requires your mind to be agile, to be able to bounce back and connect dots. This is why maintaining peak performance and balance is important.

Bill Gates, again, is well known to spend two weeks every year alone away from civilization to read, think, and get fresh ideas. He has always considered that *"you control your time. Sitting and thinking may be a much higher priority. It is not a proxy of your seriousness that you have filled every minute of your schedule."*[273]

RESPECT

In a career as a negotiator, you come across many deceptive, provocative, and disrespectful behaviors. While you may be boiling inside, you should still approach people displaying such behaviors with respect. The reason is that you never know how they will react to an offensive. I agree with Robert Greene: *"Never assume that the person you are dealing with is weaker or less important than you are. Some people are slow to take offense, which may make you misjudge the thickness of their skin and fail to worry about insulting them."*[274]

---

[271] David Comer Kidd and Emanuele Castano. "Reading Literary Fiction Improves Theory of Mind." *Science* 342(6156); (2013): 377-380.

[272] Katherine Rosman, "Bill Gates on Books and Blogging," *The New York Times*, January 4, 2016.

[273] Charlie Rose. Interview with Warren Buffett and Bill Gates. *Charlie Rose*. charlierose.com, January 27, 2017.

[274] Robert Greene, *The 48 Laws of Power* (New York: Penguin Books, 2000), 140.

In a non-official biography of Bernard Arnault, France's richest man, journalist Airy Routier explains how the condescending attitude of Arnault may have played a role in his loss of Gucci's control.

In 1991, Francois Pinault, also one of the wealthiest men in France, purchased Conforama, a large French home furnishings retail chain and property of Bernard Arnault. Arnault left the final negotiations without shaking hands with anyone or wishing the buyer good luck. Pinault commented that he had been surprised to conclude a deal with a Martian.

In 1999, LVMH gradually purchased an unwelcomed 34 percent stake in Gucci. At that time, Bernard Arnault claimed that his intention was to create a "joint venture" in which his company would help to distribute Gucci handbags and clothing around the world. Gucci's chief executive saw it as a threat and started negotiating with a white knight: Francois Pinault. Gucci convinced Pinault to subscribe new shares in Gucci and dilute the 34 percent stake of Bernard Arnault. After two years of legal battles, Arnault sold his shares in 2001 to Pinault, who ultimately took control of Gucci.[275]

The people you have disrespected can become your worse enemies lying low and waiting for the first opportunity to take revenge. They will respect you more if you respect them.

Disrespect can be expressed in the language we use, the behaviors we adopt, or the actions we take. Offensive or insensitive comments, avoidance, verbal abuse, uncivil behavior, exclusion, rude gestures, threats, yelling, harsh criticism, and so on are examples of disrespect. Let's be honest, we have all been disrespectful at some point in our life, but we need to understand that every time we show some disrespect, we reveal a weakness. This could be ignorance and a lack of confidence, empathy, or self-control. Being respectful reflects your own self-worth. There's a fine line between being firm and being offensive. It only takes one word to cross this line. Choosing to approach negotiation respectfully, avoiding arrogance and egocentrism, is opening oneself to more information, more ideas, and therefore more opportunities. Disrespectful behaviors, on the

---

[275] *L'ange exterminateur. La vraie vie de Bernard Arnault,* Airy Routier (Paris: Albin Michel, 2003).

contrary, will shut doors. Show gratitude, listen, be polite and keep a constructive attitude. Respect is a virtue, not a surrender.

AUTHENTICITY

The best definition of authenticity is given by author Amy Cuddy: *"emotions, thoughts, physical and facial expressions are in harmony. Our actions are consistent with our values. We feel that we are being true to ourselves. If our emotions are reflected in our physical expression, feel real [...] we are no longer fighting ourselves, we are ourselves."*[276]

I consider authenticity key for a negotiator as authentic people convey more confidence and trust than others. They are more easily believed than those pretending to be someone they are not. Trust starts by being true to yourself.

If you are not authentic and try too hard to hide your true nature, sooner or later it will come to the surface and people will notice. There is much more to win by getting real, softening your edges, and seeking to self-improve. Unfortunately, some like to take shortcuts. *"Nothing is more rare in any man than an act of his own. It is quite true. Most people are other people. Their thoughts are someone else's opinions, their lives a mimicry, their passions a quotation"* – such were the words of Oscar Wilde.[277]

Your character may not appeal to everyone, but it will appeal to many if your approach is genuine and your intentions are good. Your mistakes will also be more readily forgiven if you are genuine. Being an authentic negotiator doesn't mean you have to be an open book and be as transparent as fresh water. Such openness would be risky. A negotiator has to be smart and strategic about the information they share. Transparency is how much information you disclose. Authenticity is how your words, body language, and actions are aligned.

Authenticity doesn't conflict with good impressions, as the objective is still to make good ones, and not a fake one. Authenticity does not conflict

---

[276] Amy Cuddy, *Presence* (New York: Little Brown and Company, 2015), 35.

[277] *Collected Works of Oscar Wilde*, "De Profundis" (Hertfordshire: The Wordsworth Library Collection, 2007), 1084.

with change either, as an authentic person is not necessarily inflexible and can adapt to situations. On the contrary, a change of personality is a sign of inauthenticity.

One of my business partners in Asia is a switched-on grumpy single Austrian man. He is a character who sometimes lacks manners, but he is self-aware enough to genuinely apologize when he goes too far. I like and trust him because he is true to himself, he delivers, means well, and he doesn't tell me tales. He has a good network, which shows that people trust him, and a good business reputation. I know exactly what to expect from him and when he can be of great value. He never makes me waste my time, and I do my best to reciprocate.

Warren Buffet is also a good example of an authentic person. The guy has always been faithful to his values and roots without hiding them. He is friendly, truthful, humble, and close to community. He doesn't pretend to be someone he is not. He drives a simple car and eats burgers because that is what he has always done, and that is who he truly is.[278]

Inauthentic people are often afraid of being rejected. They end up struggling and stressing in search for balance. They are less emotionally stable.[279] On the contrary, authentic people are proven to be happier, calmer, open-minded, and experience more positive emotions.[280] They inspire trust more.

CHARACTER

Character is a source of power and an enhancement of a capacity to influence. It is not just a term used to describe the attributes of successful business

---

[278] Peter W. Kunhardt, *Becoming Warren Buffet*. Documentary Film. Directed by Peter W. Kunhardt. New York, NY. HBO Documentary Films, 2017.

[279] William Fleeson and Joshua Wilt, "The Relevance of Big Five Trait Content in Behavior to Subjective Authenticity: Do High Levels of Within-Person Behavioral Variability Undermine or Enable Authenticity Achievement?" *Journal of Personality*, 78:4, 1354-82. August 2010.

[280] Alison P. Lenton, Martin Bruder, Letitia Slabu, and Constantine Sedikides, "How Does 'Being Real' Feel? The Experience of State Authenticity," *Journal of Personality*, 81(3):276-289. June 2013.

leaders. It can and should form part of a negotiator's repertoire.

The Cambridge Dictionary describes character as "the particular combination of qualities in a person or place that makes them different from others." "Character" comes from old Greek kharakter which is an "engraved mark."

One of the best descriptions of a person with character is that given by David Brooks in his book titled *The Road to Character*. It actually deserves to be quoted in its entirety:

> *Occasionally, even today, you come across certain people who seem to possess an impressive inner cohesion. They are not leading fragmented, scattershot lives. They have achieved inner integration. They are calm, settled, and rooted. They are not blown off course by storms. They don't crumble in adversity. Their minds are consistent and their hearts are dependable. Their virtues are not the blooming virtues you see in smart college students; they are ripening virtues you see in people who have lived a little and have learned from joy and pain. Sometimes you don't even notice these people, because while they seem kind and cheerful, they are also reserved. They possess the self-effacing virtues of people who are inclined to be useful but don't need to prove anything to the world: humility, restraint, reticence, temperance, respect, and soft self-discipline. They radiate a sort of moral joy. They answer softly when challenged harshly. They are silent when unfairly abused. They are dignified when other try to humiliate them, restrained when others try to provoke them. But they get things done. They perform acts of sacrificial service with the same modest everyday spirit they would display if they were just getting the groceries. They are not thinking about what impressive work they are doing. They are not thinking about themselves at all. They just seem delighted by the flawed people around them. They just recognize what needs doing and they do it. They make you feel funnier and smarter when you speak with them. They move through different social classes not even aware, it seems, that they are doing so. After you've known them for a while it occurs to you that you've never heard them boast, you've never*

seen them self-righteous or doggedly certain. They aren't dropping little hints of their own distinctiveness and accomplishments. They have not led lives of conflict-free tranquility but have struggled toward maturity. They have gone some way toward solving life's essential problem, which is that, as Aleksandr Solzhenitsyn put it, 'The line separating good and evil passes not through states, not between classes, nor between political parties either—but right through every human heart.' These are people who have built a strong inner character, who have achieved a certain depth. In these people, at the end of this struggle, the climb to success has surrendered to the struggle to deepen the soul ... These are the people we are looking for.[281]

You don't need to be gifted to have character. You build character through the choices you make in life. People with character have the power to inspire others by the difference they are able to make in the development and amalgam of their abilities.

Being tough is not a trait of character. Gandhi managed to lead India's independence from Britain in 1947 promoting peaceful resistance and persistence, through powerful communication skills. Character is the result of a balanced inner force that commands respect.

The reality is that the actions of people with character are trusted more than others. These people are sought after and loved for their presence. That places them in a position to influence.

One of my clients is a true character. He is an English property developer. He is different from many successful businesspeople I know. In all our interactions over the years, I don't think I have ever seen him upset once. He is as far from being an egocentric person as anyone I've ever met. He needs not prove to the rest of the world that he is successful. He has an inner balance and the strong virtue of humility, which earns him much respect from others.

He is fit, smart, and empathic. He is calm and genuinely happy and smiling. I cannot imagine him having enemies. He always gives the impression

---

[281] David Brooks, *The Road to Character* (New York: Random House, 2015), 11.

of gliding through life, solving the problems life brings his way. He doesn't avoid conflicts; rather, he solves them gracefully. He succeeds in what he undertakes, and he accomplishes his goals, raising himself up as a course of action, while remaining always true to himself. Available, reliable, and compassionate, he is also a curious person. His way of thinking is refreshing, and discussions with him are always the most interesting. He understood early that in order to be happy and successful, one needs a solid foundation and inner balance. He grew both personal and professional successes at the same time. He closes deals and makes time for fishing in Papua New Guinea, crosses Africa with a small plane like Antoine de Saint-Exupéry, and climbs Mount Everest, all with the same zest for life. His diverse interests and activities keep him grounded. Distinctive abilities and absolute authenticity make him different and compelling.

Some people with character manage to take a step further and develop a magnetic appeal: charisma. Charisma is the result of behaviors and can be learned, eventually becoming an instinctive attribute. Great leaders are often charismatic ones. You would think that they were born with it. Yet, a majority of scientists consider that only a portion of leadership is accounted for by genetic factors (32 percent) whereas another 10 to 15 percent of it appears to be attributable to work and broader life events. The remaining 50 percent is as yet undiscovered.[282] Two-thirds of charisma and leadership is not in your genes and comes from external factors.

In *The Charisma Myth*, author Olivia Fox Cabane also considers that charisma is the result of specific behaviors. She identified 3 components showing in charismatic people (each may be stronger than another). First, behaviors of *presence*. Your body language, style, words are all aligned and converge. You are in a moment, you listen, and you are authentic. Cabane uses the example of Bill Clinton to illustrate presence. Second, behaviors of *power*. By power, she means the ability to influence the world around you through

---

[282] Richard D. Arvey, Zhen Zhang, Bruce J. Avolio, and Robert F. Krueger, "Developmental and Genetic Determinants of Leadership Role Occupancy Among Women," *Journal of Applied Technology* (2007), Vol. 92, No.3, 693-706.

money, intelligence, expertise, or status. Behaviors of power can be identified through the display of cues including posture, self-confidence, appearance, or even reaction of people around. Third, behaviors of *warmth*. It comes out of body language (eye contact, tone, opportune physical touch, etc.) and empathy.[283] I would add to the above components the ability to choose the right words. Winston Churchill would certainly be a perfect illustration.

Charismatic people often have this capacity to lead a group that people with only character don't necessarily have. They don't only inspire others, but they can captivate them.

⌈IN ESSENCE⌋

- Your image is your responsibility, and if you don't take control of it in this digital world, other people may do it for you.
- *A constant reserve is like the lock on a door which is never turned and becomes so rusty that in the end no man can open it.*
- If a good reputation should be the soil in which your personal brand is rooted, your style should be the flower.
- Do not underestimate your appearance when negotiating.
- As basic as its sounds, living a balanced life, staying in good shape, and sharpening your mind help you stay ahead of the game in the long run.
- *We are what we repeatedly do. Excellence then is not an act, but a habit.*
- You don't have to be an athlete with extraordinary abilities to reach a state of effortless concentration and efficiency. The more you throw at a flow channel, the higher your chances are to perform well and feel good about it.
- Stay calm and avoid raising defenses. You can be firm and serene at the same time.

---

[283] Olivia Fox Cabane, *The Charisma Myth: How Anyone Can Master the Art and Science of Personal Magnetism* (New York: Portfolio/Penguin, 2012).

- Patience has limits, but patience pays off better than impulsivity. Use sound judgment though and don't act blindly.
- If your mind is trained to be creative you will be more resourceful, and therefore you improve the quality of your deals.
- Read books to sharpen your mind, enhance your creativity, and enlarge your vocabulary.
- *Never assume that the person you are dealing with is weaker or less important than you are.*
- Authentic people convey more confidence and trust than others.
- You don't need to be gifted to have character. You build character through the choices you make in life.
- People with character have the power to inspire. People with charisma have the power to captivate.

CHAPTER SEVEN:

Timeless Principles

> We are drowning in information, while starving for wisdom. The world henceforth will be run by synthesizers, people able to put together the right information at the right time, think critically about it, and make important choices wisely.
>
> —Edward O. Wilson[284]

Some principles applied to negotiation are timeless. We have already tackled some of them, such as being patient and respectful, but some extend beyond personality traits. These principles have been time tested for centuries and passed from one generation to another throughout cultures. They often materialize in proverbs, stories, essays, religious texts, and so forth.

People assimilating timeless and wise principles are not only more self-aware (as wise precepts often encourage introspection) and knowledgeable, but they are also good at defining priorities and values based on experience and lessons from the past.

It is true that it is easier to accumulate wisdom through experience and information. However, enlightenment is not limited to old people (otherwise elderly would all be wise). One need not be Gandhi or the Dalai Lama to be

---

[284] Edward O.Wilson, *Consilience (New York: Vintage Books,1998), 294.*

considered wise either. Wisdom has nothing to do with intelligence. It is an attitude and a way of appreciating life and the world around.

Wise people are generally happier because they are more balanced. They have found a way to grow inside and address life's challenges. Marcus Aurelius considered that *"the happiness of your life depends on the quality of your thoughts."*[285]

Wise people know the best solution to challenging situations, while others struggle to see things clearly. They make the right choices because they see the big picture, the higher purpose, the long-term goal.

Ignoring reflections from wise thinkers and those who have already gone down your road can be a mistake. The first step to becoming wise is to act like them, and the second is to develop an ability to reflect. Remember the words of Leonardo da Vinci: *"the less you think, the more mistakes you make."*

The idea is certainly not to assimilate and apply all ancestral principles as not all of them are applicable. Rather, identify the valuable ones that can guide negotiators at any time, as lighthouses can guide navigators when they get too close to shore. Strategizing is one thing, making sound judgments is another. The amount of knowledge available to us is abundant, but wisdom is rare and priceless.

---

[285] Jeremy Collier, R. Williamson, *The Emperor Marcus Antonius: His Conversation with Himself, Together with the Preliminary Discourse of the Learned Gataker* (London: Holdorn, 1701) 155.

[29] The Power of Silence

> Oysters open completely when the moon is full; and when the crab sees one, it throws a piece of stone or seaweed into it and the oyster cannot close again so that it serves the crab for meat. Such is the fate of him who opens his mouth too much and thereby puts himself at the mercy of the listener.
>
> —Leonardo da Vinci[286]

Silence has been praised by many thinkers from Pythagoras to the Dalai Lama. Perfecting it in negotiations can be a powerful tool. We live in a world of noise where silence has almost ceased to exist to such an extent that it becomes awkward. We are surrounded by sounds (cars, planes, construction, TV, music, and so on). We also live in a world of growing impatience despite advanced transportation and time-saving tools. We do not pause enough.

Silence is uncomfortable for many people. They expect words from you more than silence. Actually, most humans cannot resist silence. Constant accessibility and exposure to background noise make a large group of us fear silence.[287] Some have calculated that the time it takes for silence to generally become uncomfortable is 4 seconds.[288]

Considering our constant need for feedback and validations, silence can quickly become destabilizing. Questions like *"Why they are not saying anything? What are they thinking about?"* will naturally come to mind.

During business negotiations, we often see negotiators leading conversations to ensure they can post all their arguments, counter-attacking any argument, or interjecting whenever a person pauses. Because they hold the

---

[286] As quoted in *The 48 Laws of Power* by Robert Greene (London: Profile Books Ltd, 2000), 33.

[287] Bruce Fell, "Bring the noise: has technology made us scared of silence?" The Conversation, December 31, 2012.

[288] Maia Szalavitz, "Awkward Silences: 4 Seconds Is All It Takes to Feel Rejected," *Time*, December 30, 2010.

floor, they think they have the upper hand. There are also situations where an employee at a meeting feels the need to speak and to shine in front of their superiors. These strategies are flawed.

Silence can be beneficial to the listener as it pushes a speaker to fill in the void, share more information, and explain in greater detail. The more a person talks, the more they run the risk of disclosing valuable information, giving clues on their strategy, if not make mistakes. Once regretful words have been put out there, it is often too late.

Silence also presents the advantage of offering an adjustment to your own language depending on what the person you converse with is disclosing. You can leverage your strategy and improve your arguments this way. It gives you time to digest the information you receive and observe body language.

You may have noticed that some master negotiators do not speak much. Why? Because they listen first, analyze, and choose their words wisely. Robert Greene wrote, *"Power is in many ways a game of appearances, and when you say less than necessary, you inevitably appear greater and more powerful than you are."*[289] It carries more weight to let everyone talk first and give an opinion at the end, with all cards in hand. The less you talk, the deeper and enigmatic you look. The Greek translation of "silence" is actually the word "mysterion," which refers to something not expressed. Silence bears mystery, which gives a hint of seduction to those who can use it wisely.

In May 1940, the Allies couldn't prevent the occupation of Norway by Hitler, and the Norwegian government sought exile to London. Although partially responsible for the disaster, 7 British destroyers were lost, plus one French and one Polish. Winston Churchill, First Lord of the Admiralty, found himself in good position to become prime minister after the fiasco. Following intense political debate and negotiations, Neville Chamberlain, prime minister at that time, held a meeting in his office attended by Lord Halifax, Churchill, and the leader and the deputy leader of the opposition Labour Party, Clement Attlee and Arthur Greenwood, respectively. Chamberlain was resigning and consulted the men in the room about who should succeed him

---

[289] Robert Greene, *The 48 Laws of Power* (London: Profile Books Ltd, 2000), 34.

as prime minister. Churchill didn't answer the question and remained silent at length, forcing Lord Halifax to break the silence and rule himself out to set the path for Churchill.[290] Churchill appeared that day as a recourse rather than an option in the eyes of the public.

Silence principles also apply to pauses between spoken sentences. These are distinct and intentional pauses rather than hesitations or disfluency. The more you pause, the better chance you have to be understood by others. If you shower a listener with words, their attention will shrink. Mark Twain once said: *"The right word may be effective, but no word was ever as effective as a rightly timed pause."*[291]

You may vary the length of your pauses to emphasize a particular subject and gain attention. Benyamin Netanyahu's speech given at the United Nations on October 1, 2015, is a good example of silence used for impact. The prime minister of Israel included these words in his speech: *"Seventy years after the murder of six million Jews, Iran's rulers promise to destroy my country, murder my people and the response from this body, the response from every one of the government representatives has been absolutely nothing, utter silence, deafening silence."* His words were then followed by 44 seconds of silence to make his point.[292] Note that pauses can help to stop a verbal attack as well and make the speaker realize that their action is inappropriate.

---

[290] Helen Cleary, "Churchill Becomes Prime Minister," British Broadcasting Corporation, March 20, 2011.

[291] Caroline Thomas Harnberger, *Mark Twain at Your Fingertips: A Book of Quotations* (Mineola, New York: Dover Publications, Inc., 2009), 520.

[292] Carol Morello and William Booth, "Netanyahu warns that Iran is building terrorist cells worldwide." *The Washington Post*, October 1, 2015.

[30] Practice Food Sharing

> The best auxiliary of a diplomat is for sure his Chef.
> —Charles-Maurice de Talleyrand-Périgord[293]

Food has always been important for humans and is not limited to a mere survival. We have shared food throughout recorded time to celebrate, show respect, make friends, or strengthen relationships. The oldest known feast would have been hosted in a cave more than 12,000 years ago in Israel.[294] The breaking of bread and the act of sharing is promoted in the Bible with bread considered as a gift from God. One of the words used to translate the word *friend* in French is "copain." Its etymology includes those who share bread together (com pain – XVIII century).

Pressured by time and cost constraints, we tend to forget that sharing food truly helps us develop rapport and gain trust from others. I sometimes see employers or business owners being unwise about it, and drastically limit their food costs. They encourage the development of relationships via phone, emails, or in an office. They underestimate the bonding effect of sharing food, sometimes obsessed by the fact that their fellows may take advantage of the situation. Limits are certainly needed, but they should not fall in the extreme of annihilating the development of precious relationships. People can be more amenable to ideas and influenced in the context of sharing food. This is why I have incorporated the organization of exclusive dinners in my business model.

---

[293] Talleyrand, Le Diable Boiteux, Secrets d'Histoire, France 2 (2012) (French translation: "Le meilleur auxiliaire d'un diplomate, c'est bien son cuisinier")

[294] Melissa Hogenboom, "Secrets of the World's Oldest Funeral Feast," British Broadcasting Corporation, May 24, 2016.

The most efficient way to negotiate with someone is not to lock them in a conference room without windows and a glass of tap water. This may be the case when a commercial agreement needs to be formalized with a team of advisors, but upstream bonding is crucial and greatly influences negotiation outcomes.

Food sharing is a nonverbal communication channel that many people are not aware of. When you share food with someone in a working environment, the relationship moves from professional toward personal. Food sharing suggests intimacy.[295] So does sharing drinks, but meals offer more structure and complexity (number of dishes, utensils, contrasts, scents, and so forth) with social codes involved such as inclusion, solidarity, or hierarchy to name a few.[296] Take for instance the act of asking a person if they would like still or sparkling water. This is a form of cooperation. These seemingly small acts facilitate the building of cohesion.

Bonding effect increases if people eat the same food or share the same dish.[297] Unconscious mimicking behavior leads to increased pro-social behavior. When individuals eat together, they unconsciously enact the same movements. This unconscious mimicking induces positive feelings toward both parties and the matter under discussion.[298]

In this context, there is a crucial question: *"Is it actually better to negotiate over a meal?"*

The *Harvard Business Review* published in 2013 an article titled "Should You Eat While You Negotiate?"[299] The author, Lakshmi Balachandra, assistant

---

[295] Lisa Miller, Paul Rozin, and Alan Page Fiske. "Food sharing and feeding another person suggest intimacy; two studies of American college students." *European Journal of Social Psychology* 28(3); (1998): 423-436.

[296] Mary Douglas, "Deciphering a Meal." *Daedalus, MIT Press,* 101(1); (1972): 61-81.

[297] "Sharing a plate of food leads to more successful negotiations," *The Economist*, March 14, 2019.

[298] Tanya L. Chartrand and Rick Van Baaren. "Human mimicry." *Advances in Experimental Social Psychology* 41. (2009): 219-274.

[299] Lakshmi Balachandra, "Should You Eat While You Negotiate?" *Harvard Business Review*, January 29, 2013.

professor at Babson College, explored *"the reasons why eating while deciding important matters increases productivity of discussions."* She observed business negotiations on MBA students in both a conference room with no food and in a restaurant. Students placed in a restaurant were able to generate more mutual benefits and profits than those in a conference room.

In 2015 researchers found we tend to be more agreeable to things while eating. Their work showed that eating a meal is associated with measurable elevations in agreeableness and reductions in dominance and submissiveness.[300]

The experience of having a good meal always puts people in a good mood and makes them feel good, while hunger makes them irritable. In this context, it is not surprising to hear that the efficient Richard Branson prefers having his meetings over a meal. In 2017 he wrote on his blog the following: *"I grab food when I can, normally scheduling a meeting over lunchtime. I'm not a fan of formal meetings and would much prefer to lighten the mood with a shared meal, or if I'm pressed for time, a walking meeting."*[301]

Diplomacy and gastronomy have always gone well together. Some call it "gastrodiplomacy." Diplomats have understood the benefits of gastronomy from time immemorial. As a matter of fact, gastronomy and diplomacy have always been closely associated. French poet Casimir Delavigne couldn't have been more correct when he wrote around 200 years ago that *"Things get worked out in the century we live in. Men are ruled through dinners."*[302]

France has been using its gastronomy as a tool in international relations for centuries. The art of serving delicate and appetizing food has long been a way for the French to showcase their know-how and excellence. Gastronomy was actually born in France with Louis XIV. This is when good cooking started

---

[300] Marije Aan het Rot, D. S. Moskowitz, Zoe Hsu, and Simon Young. "Eating a meal is associated with elevations in agreeableness and reductions in dominance and submissiveness." *Physiology & Behavior* 144(15); (2015): 103-109.

[301] Richard Branson, "My Daily Routine," Virgin.com blogpost. (https://www.virgin.com/richard-branson/my-usual-daily-routine).

[302] Oeuvres Complètes, Casimir Delavigne, (Bruxelles: Adolphe Whalen et Cie, 1838), 210. (French translation: "T*out s'arrange* en dînant dans le *siècle* où *nous sommes. Et c'est* par des *dîners qu'on gouverne les hommes"*).

to be differentiated from fine cooking ("haute cuisine"). Culinary products were enhanced to their highest level and beautifully paired. Versailles became the center of culinary excellence. Extravagant and sophisticated banquets were hosted. Francois Vatel, perfectionist majordomo, orchestrated them to perfection. For the record, the poor man ended up committing suicide to avoid disappointing Louis XIV because he came up short of seafood for one of his banquets. It seems that France has taken gastronomy very seriously from an early age.

French *"art de la table"* then moved to Paris and started to export itself, especially in the 18th century, with the objective of influencing princes and diplomats. Charles Maurice de Talleyrand-Périgord himself had the reputation of organizing beautiful and expensive dinners. He organized one of these dinners on January 3, 1798, to celebrate Napoleon, just a general at that time. Esseid Ali, the Turkish ambassador, received an invitation. The French impressed him with delicious meals and flattered him with the most beautiful women. The objective was to obtain strategic information about Egypt, which, at that time, was under Turkish administration. The rest is history. Napoleon launched a campaign the same year in Egypt. The Luxor Obelisk, which currently has pride of place in Place de la Concorde in Paris, is a reminder of that campaign.

Diplomatic dinners have always been loaded with protocols, symbols, and subtle messages, which start with the choice of venue, guest list, menu, dress code, table setting, theme, etc. They are a perfect forum for a hunger game. World leaders are so busy during the day that a chances to spend quality time with them is often limited. Therefore, protocol teams put them in the best conditions possible to optimize exchanges and generate constructive discussions.

Winston Churchill took political and diplomatic dinners to another level. Driven by his passion for wine and gastronomy, Churchill quickly realized that dinners could offer a perfect scene for his tactics. This topic is so rich in anecdotes that the author Cita Stelzer dedicated an entire book to Churchill's dinners. Here is an interesting passage:

> *Dinner parties were an important means by which Churchill rewarded friends, won over rivals and gathered information on all subjects, from diplomatic secrets to social gossip. He also hugely enjoyed them. His meals had the advantage over most other more formally scheduled encounters of being easily extended, even into the early hours of the morning, the time of day when Churchill would gather strength while others were flagging. His daughter, Mary, reports that "mealtimes tended to prolong themselves far into the afternoon or evening", with luncheons lasting until half past three or even four o'clock, and dinners going on "endlessly" after the ladies had withdrawn, to the increasing annoyance of her hostess-mother [...] Any reasonable assessment of Winston Churchill's dinner table diplomacy must conclude that we won more than he lost [...] At breakfasts, luncheons, picnics and dinners, Churchill never conformed to the Regency rules regarding the banning of politics as a proper conversational topic over meals. Instead, he would turn mealtimes into information-exchange seminars, international summits, intelligence-gathering operations, gossips fests, speech practice sessions and even semi-theatrical performances.*[303]

Many countries have now assimilated gastronomy to their diplomacy to promote local cuisine, the idea being to win hearts through stomachs. When Hillary Clinton was secretary of state, she instigated a culinary partnership with the best American chefs, using them as a resource to the State Department and offering them an opportunity to showcase American cuisine and products. Before such partnership was concluded, the State Department relied mostly on catering.[304,305] With gastronomy becoming more strategic, American statesmen may be walking in the footsteps of Thomas Jefferson,

---

[303] Cita Stelzer, *Dinner With Churchill: Policy Making at the Dinner Table* (New York: Pegasus Books, 2012) Kindle version, Loc. 228.

[304] U.S. Department of State, Notice to the Press, "State Department Launches Diplomatic Culinary Partnership," September 5, 2012.

[305] Marian Burros, "Diplomacy Travels on Its Stomach, Too," *The New York Times*, July 2, 2012.

who was well known to be a wine connoisseur travelling the vineyards of France, trying to grow vines in his Virginia estate, and organizing political dinners to develop friendships or alliances. Some of his rare bottles find their ways to auctions sometimes making them the most expensive ones ever sold in this world.[306]

When it comes to sharing food, preference should go to dinners. Although lunches, coffees, and breakfasts can work, they are more limiting and less effective. Dinners offer an informal setting far from meeting rooms, records, and minutes, which sometimes limit people's expression and honest opinions. They also offer a better chance to disconnect, and drink with moderation.

The more positive emotions you trigger at a dinner, the more memorable it will be for the person experiencing it. But the best part is that you will be associated with these memories. And trust is a step away from affinity.

Negotiators should know that food subtly affects mood, behavior, and performance.[307,308] Better food provides better fuel and keeps you naturally alert without the detriment of stimulants like caffeine.

We should all keep our wits about us when feeding our stomachs. For instance, carbohydrates, such as bread, potatoes, spaghetti, or rice, increase serotonin levels in our brain and have a relaxing effect.[309] Bitter flavors will make people more aggressive and defensive, while sweetness will make them more loving.[310] Proteins (such as meat, chicken, or fish) will keep them more

---

[306] Patrick Radden Keefe, "The Jefferson Bottles: How could one collector find so much rare fine wine?" *The New Yorker*, August 27, 2007.

[307] Ron Friedman, "What You Eat Affects Your Productivity," *Harvard Business Review*, October 17, 2014.

[308] David Perlmutter, *Grain Brain: The Surprising Truth about Wheat, Carbs, and Sugar—Your Brain's Silent Killers*, (New York:Little, Brown Spark, 2018).

[309] Andrew Smith, Susan Leekam, Ann Ralph, and Geraldine McNeill. "The influence of meal composition on post-lunch changes in performance efficiency and mood." *Appetite* 10(3); (1988): 195-203.

[310] Marta Zaraska, "Eating something sweet can lead to a romantic date." *The Washington Post*, March 28, 2016.

alert but also less calm.[311] The bottom line is that you should probably choose proteins over carbohydrates before entering any negotiation for which the stakes are high or requires attention.[312]

Once, I came across a successful American-Korean businesswoman who worked for a top branding agency in New York for many years as a high-level manager. She was well known within the company for her food strategies. She would only suggest or accept important meetings after lunch for one reason: people usually get sleepy after it and are less alert. What would she eat for lunch then? A salad and mixed fruit juice. Although I am sure she had other qualities and tactics to offer to achieve her goals, she was the highest performer in the company and managed to close a great number of deals.

Some nutritionists specialize in coaching CEOs, leaders, and entrepreneurs for a reason. Their diet can affect their mood, energy levels, and performance. But it is also a question of image. Fit leaders are viewed as more capable than overweight ones because of the assumption that weight affects health and stamina.[313] As with all factors, diet alone is not a guarantee of success in negotiation. Rather, it is part of the whole, one of these underestimated factors that can help make a difference in the end.

It is difficult to talk about sharing food and dinners without saying a few words about alcohol. Because it can be in contradiction with performance and a healthy diet, the subject is often avoided. Yet business drinking remains very much present in many cultures from first rapport established over a glass of wine to the celebration of a deal. Getting drunk can also be an important part of doing business in countries like Japan and Korea. It can be a prerequisite to trust and how business networking takes place.

---

[311] Bonnie Spring, Owen Maller, Judith Wurtman, Larry Digman, and Louis Cozolino. "Effects of protein and carbohydrate meals on mood and performance: interactions with sex and age." *Journal of Psychiatric Research* 17(2); (1983): 155-67.

[312] Jane E. Brody, "How Diet Can Affect Mood and Behavior," *International New York Times*, November 17, 1982.

[313] Leslie Kwoh, "Want to Be CEO? What's Your BMI?" *Wall Street Journal*, January 16, 2013.

Although some cultural traditions have to be respected, negotiators should avoid drinking too much alcohol as it decreases awareness and make them more exposed to mistakes and the revelation of confidential information (In Vino Veritas). Moderation should be promoted by all means in order to remain in control, especially when it comes to hard spirits. As a true champagne lover, Winston Churchill would have been caught saying one day that *"a glass of Champagne lifts the spirits, sharpens the wits, but a bottle produces the opposite effect."* It's difficult to disagree with this wisdom.

Drinking alcohol with moderation in the context of negotiation is not necessarily a bad thing, especially when it comes to wine. Unless they practice abstinence, very few people dislike wine. It can be a great icebreaker and an ally to build relationships (but probably not to agree on contract clauses or financial terms). Wine carries history, a terroir, a family, a know-how, aromas, flavors, and more. It is a story to be shared in itself.

Consumption of mild alcohol can improve creativity although it can also affect focus, and a glass of wine has a calming effect and helps the mental transition of stress to relaxation. Because we expect to be more relaxed with a glass of wine, we automatically respond by becoming more open and chattier in a subconscious attempt to meet our expectations, according to psychologists.[314,315]

---

[314] Mathias Benedek, Lisa Panzierer, Emanuel Jauk, and Aljoscha C. Neubauer, "Creativity on tap? Effects of alcohol intoxication on creative cognition," *Consciousness and Cognition* (56), November 2017: 128-134.

[315] Amy Capetta, "Science says drink up! A glass of wine can totally help chill you out," Today NBC, September 4, 2013.

⌈31⌋ Be Connected

> The richest people in the world look for and build networks. Everyone else looks for work. Marinate on that for a minute.
>
> —Robert T. Kiyosaki[316]

A good negotiator is a connected negotiator. The most influential people on this planet have a quality network. Many business opportunities, feedback, fresh ideas, and breakthroughs come from a network. The lack of a sound network can prevent one from gaining useful leverages. The old adage *"It's not so much what you know but who you know"* rings true till this day.

There has always been competition for privileged information in the history of humanity. However, more skilled people have access to it now. This drives competition for information at a faster pace. The quality of the information you get and how quickly you can get it are key to your success.

The impact of a network is greater than we think. Scientists think that we can exercise influence on any network we belong to, with up to three degrees of separation. This is what they call "social contagion." The closer people are to the center, the greater their influence on others within the network, as this is where information is shared the most.

We can shape a network, but we can also be shaped by it. A network should be curated with caution. People with negative energy or bad intentions can have an obvious or a non-obvious adverse impact on our actions.

When it comes to building a network, quality should prevail over quantity. Developing a valuable network is not limited to collecting business cards or increasing connections on our social media platforms. While social media has the great advantage of making us globally connected, only a small percentage

---

[316] Robert T. Kiyosaki, Twitter post, April 8, 2014, 2:59 PM, https://twitter.com/therealkiyosaki/status/453653343961772032?lang=

of this network has true value.

Trust still needs to be built and these contacts converted into true business opportunities. People tend to delude themselves with these superficial relationships and forget to develop true long-lasting ones. The same principle applies to attending a conference and exchanging numerous business cards. You may have broken the ice, but you have not established a solid relationship yet. You have to follow up. Some don't make this effort.

While it takes time and energy to develop trustworthy relationships, it is important to read between the lines and size people up rather quickly. Some may not have the capacity or ability to deliver what you need, and you may be wasting your time including them in your network. Very often you will meet people who will promise to do things they will not do at the end, or they will pretend they have power they don't have. Some may even play tricks on you. Learn not to chase the wrong people. Being selective with your network means bringing in people with valuable information, expertise, and connections. Seek trustworthy boosters rather than bloodsuckers.

Your network should be diversified to gather complementary people. You will collect useful opinions from different angles this way, be in a position to connect dots, and form a better perspective. The quality of your network also depends on how much effort you employ to maintain it and contribute within it. Check on people from time to time, offer to meet, provide valuable information, connections, or insights, and prioritize your connections (some people may deserve more attention than others). Keep your data updated. Never be too pushy or sound desperate.

You should select, whenever possible. intimate settings for networking. Cocktails, receptions, and conferences are not necessarily the most effective ways to develop valuable relationships as people usually try to make a positive impression and make small talk as they "work the room." Although some may be a bit chattier after a few glasses of champagne, it is rare to receive honest opinions or valuable insights at big gatherings. There is also the inevitable scenario where others will introduce themselves and potentially interrupt conversations.

[32] Be a Giver, Not a Taker

> We harvest what we have sown.
> —French proverb

Givers are more successful than takers. Self-interest, as line of conduct, exposes takers to a decrease of trustworthiness, missed opportunities, and possibly a bad reputation.

A taker is a self-serving person whose mindset conflicts with the fundamentals of negotiation, which are cooperation and compromise. By givers, I mean people who will help without waiting to be asked for it or being helped first. Givers won't expect anything specific in return. The difference between givers and takers can be illustrated by these two questions: *"what can you do for me?"* (taker) versus *"what can I do for you?"* (giver).

Statistics speak for themselves: givers deliver higher revenue in organizations in the long run, they leave a better first impression, they provide better service quality, they are more productive, and so on. Research can even predict the profitability of a corporation based on the giving rate of its employees.[317,318]

Giving may be as simple as giving feedback, making a valuable introduction, or inviting someone to dinner. *"Remember, there's no such thing as a small act of kindness. Every act creates a ripple with no logical end,"* according to cartoonist Scott Adams.[319]

---

[317] Adam Grant, "Are you a giver or a taker?" filmed at the TED Institute, November 2016. TED video, 13:13, https://www.ted.com/talks/adam_grant_are_you_a_giver_or_a_taker/.

[318] Nathan P. Podsakoff, Steven W. Whiting, and Philip M. Podsakoff. "Individual- and Organizational-Level Consequences of Organizational Citizenship Behaviors: A Meta-Analysis." *Journal of Applied Psychology*, 94(1); (2009): 122–141.

[319] Scott Adams, "27 Quotes About Kindness for World Kindness Day (and Every Day)," *Parade* (online), November 13, 2018.

Being a giver is not being too nice or blindly accepting all contract terms. No one should be a people-pleaser. It is more a question of showing good and genuine intentions to people who matter. It is possible you get nothing in return, but you are playing the long-term game, and you are not there to charge every minute you spend with these people. Worse scenario is that you will improve the way others view you. Most people remember these acts of kindness and the law of reciprocity may naturally play in your favor. Giving helps build relationships. It shows you care and that you are giving people attention.

I believe in the adage *"What goes around comes around."* I also believe that you can't climb very high on the backs of others, and that you may fall quickly.

[33] Keep Your Promises

We promise according to our hopes; we fulfill according to our fears.
—François de La Rochefoucauld[320]

Keep your word, even it is expensive and inconvenient. Your word is your true worth. We all meet overcommitters. They are nice and optimistic, convinced they can help, and then nothing happens. They want to please others, look good, or gain trust too quickly. They underestimate the cost of their promises, or they just stop making effort if they no longer benefit. Then they claim a lack of time or an unforeseen event to justify their inaction. Some may not even bother apologizing and will become amnesic. Jean-Jacques Rousseau saw it clearly: *"Those that are most slow in making a promise are the most faithful in the performance of it."*[321]

---

[320] François de La Rochefoucauld, *Reflections; or Sentences and Moral Maxims* (New York: Scribner, Welford and Co., 1871), 7.

[321] *Émile, ou de l'éducation* (Paris: Charpentier, 1848) 486. (French translation: "Le plus lent à promettre est toujours le plus fidèle à tenir")

Keeping your word is actually valued more by others than exceeding your promises.[322] Negative experiences stick more and longer in the minds of people. We have all experienced this disappointment when someone says they will call back but don't, or they will make an introduction and they don't. Because they don't feel immediate consequences or are in a powerful position, they don't feel guilty and refuse to question themselves. They don't realize that their reputation is eroding like the base of a cliff slowly deteriorated by waves (and I am not talking about bigger promises that, when not kept, can have a devastating effect). Apologies won't totally fix them, especially if it is not the first time it happens, or if breaking the promise generates a loss or damage.

It is better to make fewer promises and keep them all. If you are unsure you can keep your word, do not offer it. How do you want to build trust with others if you don't do what you say? It is counterproductive. Make promises but keep them, even small ones, and you will be better trusted. Yes, it can cost you to keep your word, it may take more of your time or stress you out, but your image won't be tarnished this way.

Not keeping your word is not necessarily being dishonest. You may have genuinely overpromised something or just been forgetful. Memory slips can be explained in different ways, including stress, which prevents one from being focused, and lack of sleep.[323] Don't overextend yourself, and keep yourself balanced and healthy to avoid those slips.

Research shows that corporations and leaders who keep their promises generate better returns, are more productive and profitable, and develop better relationships. They also have a higher level of attractiveness.[324]

---

[322] Ayelet Gneezy and Nicholas Epley. "Worth Keeping but Not Exceeding: Asymmetric Consequences of Breaking Versus Exceeding Promises." *Social Psychological and Personality Science* 5, no. 7 (September 2014): 796–804.

[323] Howard LeWine, M.D., "Too little sleep, and too much, affect memory," Harvard Health Blog, October 29, 2015.

[324] Luigi Guiso, Paola Sapienza, and Luigi Zingales. "The Value of Corporate Culture." (September 1, 2013). *Chicago Booth Research Paper* No. 13-80; Fama-Miller Working Paper.

⌈IN ESSENCE⌋

- Wisdom has nothing to do with intelligence and age. It is an attitude and a way of apprehending life and the world around.
- *The happiness of your life depends on the quality of your thoughts.*
- Practice silence to push speakers to fill in the void, share more information, and explain in greater detail. Adjust your own language based on what the person you converse with is disclosing.
- The less you talk, the deeper and enigmatic you look.
- The more you pause the better chance you have to be understood by others.
- A good negotiator is a connected negotiator. The most influential people on this planet have a quality network.
- The impact of a network is greater than you think. The closer you are to the center, the greater your influence.
- Quality of a network should prevail over quantity.
- Size people up with accuracy quickly. Seek trustworthy boosters rather than bloodsuckers.
- Be a giver. Self-interest, as line of conduct, exposes takers to a decrease of trustworthiness, missed opportunities, and possibly a bad reputation.
- *Remember, there's no such thing as a small act of kindness. Every act creates a ripple with no logical end.*
- *What goes around comes around.*
- You can't climb very high on the backs of others, and you may fall quickly.
- Keep your word, even it is expensive and inconvenient. Your word is your true worth and is valued more by others than exceeded promises.
- By constantly not keeping your promises, you erode your reputation like the base of a cliff slowly deteriorates with waves.

I hope you have enjoyed this book
and that you have found it interesting and informative.
I would appreciate if you could leave a review on:

AMAZON:
www.amazon.com

BARNES & NOBLE:
www.barnesandnoble.com

GOODREADS:
www.goodreads.com

Thank you!

LUDOVIC TENDRON is a successful influencer, business strategist, entrepreneur, and lawyer. He is the founder of Ludovic®, a business development advisory firm, and the co-founder of Vitisasia®, a lifestyle platform offering exclusive wine and gastronomic experiences as an effective forum for business networking.

Fueled by his curiosity and the pursuit of peak performance, Ludovic set upon a multi-year journey to research the modern science behind negotiation and influence by exploring the deeper roots of human nature. What started as a study for his personal interest and that of his clients developed into *The Master Key: Unlock Your Influence & Succeed in Negotiation*, a comprehensive and indispensable guide that provides a perspective and insights of a master negotiator.

Ludovic offers groundbreaking speaking engagements and corporate training on enhancing one's ability to negotiate and influence people. Ludovic lives between Asia and France with his wife and daughter. He also is a strong supporter of environmental causes.

Ludovic
.online

NEGOTIATION WORKSHOPS

Tailored for Executives
Microexpression Exercises
Powerful Roleplays & Take-aways
Overlooked Performance Factors

info@ludovic.asia
+65 9786 6484

Printed in Great Britain
by Amazon